Offensive Line Philosophies & Line Play

Michael Lavelle

My face is set, my gait is fast, my goal is Heaven, my road is narrow, my way is rough, my companions are few, my guide is reliable, my mission is clear. I cannot be bought, compromised, diluted or delayed, I will not flinch in the face of sacrifice, hesitate in the presence of adversity, negotiate…at the table of the enemy, ponder at the pool of popularity, or meander in a maze of mediocrity. I won't give up, shut up, let up, or slow up.
-Robert Moorehead

Contents

Philosophy..1
Blocking, (Base)..2
    At the Line of Scrimmage...3
Blocking Techniques..3
Techniques Versus...5
Various Blocks...6
Blocks..6
    Drive..6
    Reach...6
    Cutoff...7
    Full Man Cutoff..7
    Cut...8
    Back/Down..8
    Chip (Bump)...9
    Pulling...9
    Crab..10
    Butt...11
    Combo/Zone..11
    Zone Combo (Inside/Outside)...13
    ½ Man..15
Pass Protection..16
    Fundamentals..16
    At the Line Of Scrimmage..16
    Punch Points..17
        Line Awareness, (Introduction)..18
        Versus Head-up...19
        Versus Inside...19
        Versus Outside..20
Line Awareness Points..20
Line Awareness...23
        Set-up..25
        Sets vs. Alignment...26
        Drill...27
Three Man Rules..28
        Reads..29
Slide Protection..30
Sprint-out Protection..31
Tight Ends in Protection..32
Counters..32
        Versus Rip..33
        Versus Swim..33
        Versus Bull...33
        Versus Push-Pull..34
        Versus Club..34
O-Line Toolbox..34
Blocking Line Stunts..35
Tight End Releases..37
PAT/Field Goal..38

Philosophy

I. Develop football intelligence-a complete understanding of the position as well as the game itself, in addition to what is trying to be accomplished. Unit attitude is a direct reflection of its coach and motto.
   A. Example
      Run Game-
         a. Who is carrying the ball?
         b. Where is the point of attack?
         c. What is the design of the play (fast or slow)?
         d. What is my angle of departure?
      *When all is understood it will automatically be known what techniques are needed and with whom will you be working with.
   B. Pass Game-
         a. Where is the release point?
         b. What is the backfield action?
         c. How much time is needed?
         d. What is the scheme?
         e. Where is help coming from?
         f. What are my Line Awareness points?
   C. Critical Points-
         a. Understanding your role
         b. Mistakes
         c. Mental errors
         d. Physical errors
         e. Penalties
         f. Decrease your margin for error
         g. Promote self-improvement
         h. Film study, study sheets, test, and pre-practice

II. Constantly evaluate my coaching techniques.
   A. Classroom-
         a. Differences in teaching and learning
         b. Board, overhead projector, visual aides
         c. Is it all being clearly conveyed
         d. Understand the progression and goal
         e. Have the players re-teach it
         f. Create scenarios
         g. Delivery-clear and concise

III. Coaching Techniques.
   B. On the field-
         a. Always be prepared to answer why and what if

b. Never lie and don't B.S.-if you don't know be honest and get the answer immediately, never leave it hanging unless that is a solution
   c. Set the attitude and expectations for practice-keep it demanding, upbeat, goal-oriented, intense
   d. Maximize all allotted times designated for teaching
   e. Spend enough time that is needed for what needs to be done
   f. Formulate your plan for the entire week and what needs to be addressed
   g. Mesh Quality and Quantity drill work for what is necessary, mix it up and keep it fresh
   h. Never stop teaching, coaching, communicating
   i. Coach every player, speak to every player
   j. Know your players and what they need to be successful
   k. When a player leaves the field he should leave a better player than the day before
C. Game Day-
   a. Have prepared adjustments ready for potential problems
   b. Maintain excellent communication with players and coaches
   c. Maintain a positive mental edge during all adjustments and series
   d. Ensure feedback and adjustments are understood by all players
   e. Create an atmosphere around the unit that is energizing, intense, contagious, inviting
   f. Have fun and expect the unexpected

Blocking

Progression:
   a. Base-shoulder width or slightly wider (can vary).
   b. Feet-slight stagger (can vary) with inside foot up-toe to instep or tighter. Toes pointing slightly outward while knees are aligned with position of the feet (can vary). Feet flat with heels staying light by weight shifted slightly to the balls of the feet.
   c. Power Angles-knee of the up foot directly under the chest muscle creates a 'Z' shape to ankle and knee joints. Weight rolled up forward slightly over the knee of the up foot. A strain of the upper and outer quads should be felt.
   d. Set Position-from the 2pt stance our forearms touch the thigh pads-hands are slightly tight ready to punch. This automatically puts them in a clenched position. Another variation of technique is to place the hands above the knee between the thumb and index finger. In a 3pt stance the down hand is placed under the chin with mild weight applied on the fingertips. This hand should be able to move without altering the balance of the player. The opposite hand can be clenched and placed outside the knee or cupped over the top of the knee

between the thumb and index finger. Foot positioning and balance does not change unless technically needed and shall only be slight.
e. Back is slightly arched in a 2pt and flat in a 3pt. Shoulders remain square to the line of scrimmage.
f. From a 2pt-tail is slightly back and tense while position can vary. A 3pt has it even with the shoulders.
g. Head up, chest out, with the eyes looking both ways before locking forward.

Drill- Spread out facing same direction, practice technique and check for flaws.
Remedy-Video/Mirror

At the L.O.S

Split-Base rule is two-three foot split. Splits adjusted by design of the play or technical advantage. Guards will align their toes of their inside foot to heels of the Center (will vary.) Tackles will align evenly with the guards. Tight end will follow playside Tackle. This positioning too will be used to our advantage. All alignments will change by field position, personnel and down and distance.

Stance-Should never be comfortable, however, it should be balanced, steady, and read to uncoil, maintaining a slight stagger with the feet (will vary). A strain should be felt in the upper and outer quads. Weight should always be centered then altered to our advantage. For example, preparing yourself to pull, by this you place an adjusted amount of weight on the foot by which you'll be pivoting. All adjustments are to be minute without showing your intentions. If the stance is poor then one is almost certainly guaranteed to fail at their assignment. Right side of the line places their right hand down while the left places their left. If Tackle has a TE next to him he is down in a 3pt stance while the Tackle away is up in a 2pt. If DE is outside TE then Tackle is up in a 2pt stance. Guards will be in a 3pt unless the situation dictates otherwise.

Take-off and Angles of Departure-An offensive lineman departs from the line of scrimmage one of three ways when run blocking and depending on his assignment as well as the positioning of the man he needs to block. Pulling is an exception to this rule. There are three angles of departure-T-board (Power), Flat (Swift), and Bucket (Check). These types of departures are used for one-on-one blocks and combo blocks for the zone scheme and man scheme.

Drill-Boards

Blocking Techniques
One-on-One
Versus a Head-up-(T-Board) **Step 1-**is a quick step with the playside foot of the call side. It is to cover (align with) up the defenders widest foot, by this he is covered up. Hips should remain loose and the step should not be too wide or too

tight. This step is about timing and placing you in the perfect position for your punch, base, and finish. * Aiming point-eyes to the chin.

Step 2-is a power step, up the middle of the cylinder for wide plays, inside his inside foot, for inside plays. Get it flat on the ground quickly (pick up real estate) but don't over extend, contact will be simultaneous with this step.

Contact on step 2-must be made with tremendous force (punch) and exactness. This is also known as explosion at the point of attack or P.O.A. It is imperative to get leverage at this point and thus maintain it. This is a technical step by which when performed correctly significantly increases the chances for success.

After a perfect get off and approach, comes the punch with both hands, which once again needs to be violent and explosive. When done correctly it will stun the defender and position him at a point where you can follow through with your remaining steps. The punch should be inside the arms of the defender with your thumbs tight and in the up position (snatch technique). A great aiming point is the piece of shoulder pad inside the armpit covering the chest. Shoulders and triceps should be flexed or squeezed, so they will uncoil with the force needed. Elbows tucked in with shoulders and hips remaining lower then his to ensure and maintain leverage. Uncoiling must be done without winding up or bringing your elbows back; it needs to be harnessed from the power that is generated by the kinetic energy of the previous techniques. Toes are slightly pointed out with your weight distributed evenly but emphasized on the inner halves of your feet. Knees are slightly inward. The drive then becomes short choppy steps (app. 4-6") to pick up real estate that remain flat footed while maintaining power angles. Keep the defender covered up. Anticipate an initial stalemate, so do not break technique, keep leverage and we will win.

Step 3- Rolling off the Firm-As anticipated when steps 1 and 2 are done correctly there will be a slight stalemate. This is where success is achieved. Ground that second step and roll the knee of that foot over the toe. You are now straining to get the third step down. Continue this for the next step or until you move to the finish aspect of the block. If the block becomes more difficult or the stalemate increases then just drop the knee lower and continue on. If your initial hand placement is lost then sumo for better hand position.

Finish-After the initials steps are done, maintain leverage and strain up the defender, roll your hips under your shoulders, and lift him from his shoes as you finish the drive. Climb and make this finish as violent and demoralizing as possible. You can physically abuse and ware him down. As your rolling out of the block increase the speed of your steps and punch and push. When the defender adjusts to the ball or reaches out, drive and finish on top with a pancake. For outside blocks utilize the Steer Technique.

Helmet Placement-is of paramount importance. Always keep your helmet between the defender and the ball. A good block doesn't necessarily mean that your face needs to make contact. However, for certain blocks, to initially get leverage 3pt contact is necessary.

Techniques Versus

Inside Shade-2i, 4i, 6i-step with the inside foot first. The alignment of the defender will dictate the depth of your initial step.

Head-up-0, 2, 4-step with the playside foot of the call side first. This will be a T-board step. At times and depending on the player as well as play, a change of technique can be employed. A Flat step can be used. This is an excellent approach versus a swimmer.

Outside Shade-3, 5, 7, 9, wide 5-This step is the Bucket step and its depth depends on the width of the defender. The wider he is the more depth you get with the first step.

Aiming Point-(Point of Attack) Depends on the play called.
When the P.O.A is inside, work the inside number to inside armpit.
When the P.O.A is over you, work the inside of the outside number.
When the P.O.A is outside, work the outside number to outside armpit.

Note: With the variations of the shade and the exception of step 1, all remaining steps or finish are the same. When the situation is combo blocking adjustments are made by design of the play and alignment of the defender or defenders.
Keys:
- Communication
- Technique
- Explosion at the P.O.A (Intensity)
- Rolling off the firm (Strain)
- Maintain Leverage
- Finish, Finish, Finish

Drill: Stance and start-step 1
One-two-punch step 2
Go-2-go-   step 3
Full go   All blocks

Thought:-Offensive line play is immensely detail oriented and requires a tremendous amount of self-discipline. It's a combination of hand-to-hand combat and wrestling. Everything done is done by progression and must be served with intensity, desire, and an aptness to demoralize your opponent. This of course is done well within the legal boundaries of the game. Run blocking is absolutely about attitude and leads all other determining factors that encompass it.
This is a special position that requires a unique player.

Various Blocks-
1. Drive
2. Reach
3. Cutoff
4. Cut
5. Back
6. Down
7. Chip (Bump)
8. Pulls-Trap, Wrap, Boot, G scheme tight/wide
9. Crab
10. Combos
11. ½ Man (Double)
12. Recovery (Butt)

Drive Block-

Function: Is the basic run block.

Attack Point: The initial step is determined by the alignment of the defender and the play called. A defender can only line-up in a certain number of places, therefore our departure will be one of the three ways:

T-Board (Power) vs. Head-up-Covered
Flat (Swift) vs. Tight Shade- In/Out
Bucket (Check) vs. Wide defender-Uncovered/Covered
Progression: Stated earlier

Reach Block-

Function: To block a defender in an outside technique, relative to the P.O.A.

Attack Point: Playside, inside outside number to outside armpit.

Progression:
Step1- Bucket step depending on the width of the defender. The ankle of the foot stepping first needs to be outside of the knee. Outside toe aims at the defenders outside foot. Get eyes to the target immediately.

Step 2- Second step is down the middle of the defender and needs to be quick, with simultaneous punch. *With an outside technique to the call side aim for the outside number with the inside shoulder or flipper. Align your inside ear and hip to his outside ear and hip.

Step 3- Maintain leverage with a strong base, arms and hands remain strong fighting for outside leverage. Hips should not swing but rather be in a perfect position to move out and up working towards 45°. Do not be soft as to allow penetration and helmet placement should align with hips.

Finish: Continue with outside leverage as you climb to the next level.

Note: If defender jumps or gets outside leverage then finish remaining drive block with steer technique.

Drills: (See manual), Drive progression, boards, bags, sled, and acceleration.

Cutoff Block- *Find videos*

Function: To stop penetration and pursuit and to seal backside penetration and cross face pursuit by a down defender. Toughest assignment when the defender is shaded to the call side.

Attack Point: against an inside shade towards the call side, is his inside hip.
Progression:
Step 1-Drop step (Bucket)-depending on width.

Step 2-Quick step and rip to get over and get hips and body aligned. Do not cross feet here or take a large second step, it will result in immediate penetration and the defender deflecting off your attempt. It is imperative to get the rip (flipper) with your outside arm across his inside number as the second step hits the ground. Your shoulders must be lower than his for leverage.

Step 3-Now your outside foot becomes your up foot, maintain a strong base, with a good lean keep your inside arm free to use as leverage.

Note: If its not made right away just keep working that angle while pitter pattering your feet. Conversely, if perfect position is achieved without much fight, slow down and keep progression. If you lose positioning work a butt block.

Attack Point: against an outside shade away from the call side, is his inside number.
Progression:
Step 1-Depends on the defenders style and technique, will be a hard flat step or short drop step with your inside foot; keeping your ankle outside the knee.

Step 2-Quick step is grounded inside of his inside foot maintaining leverage with a strong squared base. Contact the attack point using your outside arm with a flipper or if necessary solid punch.

Step 3-With great positioning; maintain a strong drive block (1/2 man).

Note: If the defender plays you hard just drive him and finish. If he plays soft or stays wide, just get a hard jab and climb to level 2.

Full Man Cutoff-

Function: Block a defender one full man over.
Attack Point: Inside of the outside number of defender aligning eyes and nose to outside armpit.

Progression:
Step 1-Step with the inside foot pulling flat down the line (Deep bucket).

Step 2-Quick step to align position with leverage for slight climb. Attack the inside of the outside number with Lazy shoulder or inside flipper while locking eyes to the target. Upon contact, rip with the inside arm only half way to allow for a maximum fit with leverage. Any higher increases the chances to lose leverage by the way of your body becoming extended.

Step 3-Work to maintain perfect position out and up by aligning inside ear and hip to his outside ear and hip. When backside, utilize the butt block if needed.

Note: If necessary and block becomes unattainable then perfect place to cut (backside), or rip and club (inside steer and playside) with the inside arm at his inside tricep to thrust him past and allow for cutback.

Drills: (See manual), Boards, bags, acceleration, ½ and full line.

Cut Block-
Function: To cut the legs out from a defender neutralizing him in his place.

Attack Point: Varies slightly for a fast moving (LB) or slow moving (DL) defender. Attack point is the same but you must account for the difference of speed. Target is mid thigh of the playside leg.

Progression:
Step 1-Depending on the style and technique of the defender, drop step or slight bucket.
Step 2-Quick step is down and inside, positioning the body to explode by uncoiling off the line while shooting the arm opposite playside between the legs and behind the knee while attacking with that same shoulder. Head remains up at all times. Be sure to land clean.

Step 3-If the defender reads it or plays off of it then maintain the block by driving on all fours.

Note: Always anticipate the defenders movement and adjust accordingly. Versus a linebacker keep your eyes on the attack point and explode through about one step in front. Once the cut is made get up and continue on blocking.

Drills: Bags, downfield open space on bags, boards vs. LB's, *DL jump vs. pass.

Back/Down Block-
Function: To block a defender inside or seal an area vacated by a pulling lineman.
Attack Point: Depends on the style and technique of the defender. Attack point is initially the same but it adjusts if the defender changes his approach. Target the playside number to opposite armpit.

Progression: Versus a <u>Penetrator</u>-

Step 1-Depends on the defenders alignment and technique, short drop step or slight bucket; aimed at his inside toes but spaced enough to put yourself in perfect position.

Step 2-Quick step is firmly put down aiming at the defenders near hip. A violent punch is right up through the numbers and that immediate area of the rib cage to armpit. Helmet is aligned with the hips and placed in a position in front to negate his thrust.
Step 3-Finish remaining drive block without allowing penetration.

<u>Versus a Reader</u>-

Step 1-Remains the same.

Step 2-Remains the same but here you will identify his reaction and adjust accordingly. When you feel his passivity you must now redirect by shorting your attack point and moving your helmet placement behind him or up field.

Step 3-Finish remaining drive block up field.

Note: If the defenders pre-snap alignment is tight, your first step becomes a short lead step.

Drills: Boards, bags, ½ and full line schemes.

Chip Block-
Function: To partially block a defender through a combo scheme (bump), while blocking to level 2, or for (TE) baiting and blocking area to allow a quick release.

Attack Point: Near Shoulder.

Progression:
Step 1-Depends on defenders alignment, with whom you're working with, and design of the play. Lead step with the foot that will enable contact and punch (flipper) by the second step. * A gallop or short repeat step will be utilized to close the space if it exists between the 1st and 2nd step prior to contact.

Step 2-Quick step with a strong base, deliver a violent flipper or punch; anticipate a spike.

Step 3-When passed off or a successful chip is made continue on to level 2 or (TE) remaining assignment.

Drills: Zone, acceleration, ½ and full line schemes.

Pulling-Trap, Wrap, Boot, G scheme-tight/wide

Function: To vacate an area and either lead block, seal block, fold block or isolate a defender.

Attack Point: When down the L.O.S it's always best to maintain an in-to-out relationship with your helmet up field while attacking with your initial inside shoulder. Right side uses left shoulder while left side uses right shoulder. When defender is 2 yards in the hole and outside, attack through his inside number and kick out. If defender is up field attack him as if down the L.O.S. If he is in the hole and inside, log and seal inside by driving your helmet to his outside number and rotating your hips and shoulders while maintaining a strong base. Do this unless play design dictates otherwise.

Progression:
Step 1-Pre-snap stance must be balanced with slight weight emphasized on the pivoting foot. If it's a tight pull then lead with a short firm step into the line and if it's a wide pull such as wrap or boot then take a deeper drop or exaggerated bucket. Do not over extend. Pick up real estate on the first step. If it's a cross scheme, take a 1/2 bucket step while placing your 2nd step up towards the hole or vacated area. If it's a Tight G (-2 gaps) then sling step it with eyes locked on assignment (LB). This is done by leading back with the foot away from the scheme while the second step gathers and aligns. Wide G (+2 gaps) follows pulling rules.

Step 2-Quick step to recover body position and align yourself on the proper angle. Whip your playside arm out for leverage and momentum, however, keep it controlled.

Step 3-Maintain a strong demeanor as you eye your target, playing with a lean and leverage. Contact should be violent as you punch while rolling your hips driving your feet keeping a wide base.

Note: When passing through the L.O.S on a long pull, your shoulders should nearly be square. If target is lost keep eyes to the inside; don't pass up a color. Use your face to dictate position on a fast moving linebacker. Be sure to look both ways pre-snap. Technical differences can be found by using a play side lead step for boot and leading back with the inside/outside foot on folds or tight G schemes.

Drills: (See manual), Power, trap, 1&2 gap pull.

Crab Block-
Function: To attack a defender, on either call side for quick hitting plays.

Attack Point: Similar to the cut, this block is targeted above the knee to the call side. Ideal hand placement is grounded inside the leg to the call side.

Progression:
Step 1-Depends on the defenders alignment and style. Short lead step targeted at the playside foot.

Step 2-Quick step is down and inside, positioning the body to explode by uncoiling off the line while shooting the hands towards the attack point and attacking with the shoulder opposite playside. Head remains up. Contact at this point is made on or while in transition to all fours.

Step 3-If the defender reads it then maintain the block by driving on all fours while adjusting your hips. Keep your hips low enough for smoother transition.

Butt Block-
Function: See cutoff block. In addition used as a recovery tool for lost positioning during pass protection.

Drills: Bags, partner, line awareness.

Combo Blocks/Zone Blocks-
Function: To get vertical movement on a down defender using 2 offensive linemen, thus creating a greater run surface while attacking stacked or flowing linebackers. Combo Blocks roll into inside/outside zone blocking and can be emphasized as building a wall as well as creating cutback lanes by negating pursuit between the tackles.

Zone Combo Calls: Tate=Tackle and Tight End (Playside)
                      Tag=Tackle and Guard (Playside)
                      Cog=Center and Guard (Playside)
                      Scoop=Center and Guard (Backside)
                      Slip=Tackle and Guard (Backside)
                      Slate=Tight End and Tackle (Backside)

Note: Add "-IT" to the call, takes you to the backer away from call side. (Wrap, Power scheme) Add "-O" to the call, takes you to the backer outside to the call side. (Outside Zone scheme) Used by the TE and Tackle. Add "I" to the call, takes you to the backer inside. There will be instances in zone where more than 2 offensive linemen are used (Grease/Oil).

"Oil"-Is an alert called by the PST; means 3-man zone vs. a Stick or Dbl Stick stunt. "Oil-Lock"-Is an alert call by the PST that tells PSG/C that stunt can be on-so PST/PSG stay solid while uncovered takes best path to level 2 (varies by front).

"Slick"-Is an Oil alert called by the PST with no TE; it tells the PSG/C that the PST will allow the end to come clean vs. a "Stick/slant" therefore allowing PSG/C a clearer path to the 2nd level. *PST must be aggressively <u>soft</u>.

Attack Point: Depends on the defenders alignment, call side of the play, and whose is working together. Who is covered and uncovered? Initially is the run designed to go inside or outside?

Explanation of Point:
The combo, double team, and zone blocks are all relatively the same; however, there are technical differences, which must be understood. It depends on the defenders alignment, play called (inside/outside); whom you are working with, and are you covered or uncovered? Once all is known, then your approach will be either the post blocker or drive blocker. The post blocker (covered man) follows through with his normal progression, while the drive blocker (uncovered) will adjust accordingly. For inside zone, the post blocker will use the flipper or 3pt punch to maintain playside leverage. For combo and double teams he looks to attack by exploding the near shoulder while aligning hip to hip, and getting vertical movement. Targeted to get to level 2, both the post blocker and the drive blocker react to the down defenders movement. The drive blocker will key the defenders near hip, pit, and shoulder (towards or away from him) while the post blocker stays his course. Uncovered, works for playside leverage while pushing the covered off to the next level. Covered establishes and maintains playside leverage while working to the next level. If the down defender spikes towards the uncovered, he will adjust and drive while the post blocker will punch down, tighten and get eyes immediately to level 2. For outside zone, all linemen step playside and depending on the defenders alignment will adjust their technique and attack point. It is imperative to not allow a gap or crease to form between the covered and uncovered for either scheme thus allowing the defender to split our zone. Keep movement outside and up.

Progression:
Combo Block-

Aiming Point- (Target Area)-(Point of Attack) Depends on the play called.
When the P.O.A is inside, work the inside number to inside armpit.
When the P.O.A is over you, work the inside of the outside number.
When the P.O.A is outside, work the outside number to outside armpit.

Covered-
Step 1-T-Board or Flat depends on defenders alignment.
Step 2-Quick step, violent punch. When Flat stepping, aiming point is under defenders numbers with your face point to the outside for leverage.
Step 3-Work to maintain playside leverage and finish drive block.

Uncovered-
Step 1-Flat step slightly up and in to defender.
Step 2-Quick step, attack defenders near shoulder getting it to lift and turn.
Step 3-Get hip-to-hip and finish drive block.

Note: Keep hip-to-hip relationship utilizing point-pec, under, or palm technique. Proper angle of departure prepares for any stunt combo. Eyes on down defender to level 2; do not climb out until vertical movement has been achieved. If down defender attacks the uncovered then he assumes the drive while the covered works body position and vertical movement eying level 2.

Double Team-
Covered-Same as combo steps

Uncovered-Same as combo steps
Notes: Technical variations will be employed versus tight or "it" doubles, by utilizing modified (common) leg steps with point-pec, under, or palm technique.

Zone Combos

Zone Block Inside-

Covered-
Step 1-Take a play side lead step either T-Board or Flat depending on defenders alignment. *Aiming point varies based on alignment, inside to outside across the numbers relative to the P.O.A (see aiming point-target area).
Step 2-Quick step down, 3pt punch or flipper the nearest shoulder to armpit. *Utilize the 3pt punch based upon the style of the defender relative to the P.O.A. This occurs by attacking the shoulder nearest playside with a fist to point with the playside arm while utilizing the flipper (wrist to pit) or point palm with the opposite. **When just using the flipper, be sure to utilize the opposite arm for leverage and separation while securing the defender into a fit.

Step3- Eyeing level 2; maintain drive when pushed off attack level 2 linebacker with 3pt contact to center mass with the snatch technique. If defender slants outside and is in your path lock on and finish normally.

Uncovered-
Step 1-Bucket step; depth depends on defenders alignment. Eyes to the near hip, pit, and shoulder. Target area is eyes to the middle of the inside number. *The tighter the defender is to the uncovered the tighter the aiming point becomes; conversely the wider he is, the wider it becomes. This ensures that the uncovered will take the proper depth to get where he needs to go.
Step 2-Quick step down; punch, work to maintain playside leverage.
Step 3-If attacked work positioning and drive, if not work to release covered on level 2.
*Expect contact and decision for down defender between 3 and 4 steps, while contact to LB is 3 to 5 steps depending on the play of the down man and D-scheme.

Zone Block Outside-
Covered-
Step 1-Depends on the defenders alignment, T-board, Flat, or slight Bucket. This step is taken to work for immediate outside leverage. If outside; take a Bucket for

width; Flat and up for head-up; and T-board for inside. *Aiming point varies based on alignment, inside to outside shoulder across the numbers relative to the P.O.A.

Step 2-Quick step; depth depends on defenders alignment- flipper or punch through for inside to head-up technique. Work to maintain outside leverage while turning the defenders shoulder. Do this by aligning inside ear and hip to his outside ear and hip. If shade is outside, attack the outside of the outside number with a lazy shoulder while shooting the outside fist (point to pit) at the playside shoulder while locking eyes to the target. *If working a with partner inside; the defender slants in, then graze and pass off. Upon contact rip with the inside arm only half way to allow for a maximum fit with leverage. Any higher increases the chances to lose leverage by the way of your body becoming extended.

Step 3-Square up eyeing level 2; maintain drive when pushed off attack level 2 linebacker with 3pt contact utilizing the playside outside arm to obtain leverage. When the defender spikes inside, don't chase, rather graze and pass off; attack the next defender or level immediately.

Key point: Utilize communication. Do not chase inside unless scheme dictates, yet be sure to not allow a crease to develop.

Uncovered-
Step 1-Bucket step; depth depends on defenders alignment. Target area is-outside number to pit through the middle of both numbers eying the near hip, pit, and shoulder.

Step 2-Quick step; punch playside number to shoulder to work for outside leverage. If attacked, transition hips keeping helmet playside then continue with drive progression.

Step 3-Finish the drive working up field while pushing the covered off on to level 2. If uncovered path takes you directly to the next level, then attack flowing linebacker with shoulders slightly bladed therefore allowing the back to see color enabling a reaction. If your path cuts the LB off then crush and seal inside.

Note: All steps and finishes are the same for drive progression. Technical differences are made based on the down defenders alignment, play design, and call side. A good habit to develop when stepping is utilizing zone indicators (arms), by which establishes separation and presence. When blocking outside, if defender jumps or gets outside leverage then finish remaining drive block with steer technique.

Drills: (See manual) Zone vs. 1/2/3, ½ line, full line.

Steer Technique-Is an excellent technique when run blocking outside to the call side and if the defender has front side leverage or is dragging yet still fighting for it. It serves pressure to counter pressure and when employed correctly is immediately effective. Upon an excellent set, punch, fit, and drive; as the defender is fighting the pressure to keep outside leverage, he will naturally put more emphasis on his outside arm. When this is felt; from inside control the lineman will lock his outside arm and punch up and through with his inside arm while driving on the angle.

Result: shoulders of defender should immediately blade thus negating his leverage and base facilitating a pancake.

Drills: Acceleration, down the line w/ in/out control, 1-2 arm progression.

½ Man Block-

Function: Used primarily in zone schemes; serves as the base principle for the covered or front side lineman. This is done to maintain play side leverage.
Attack Point: Nearest shoulder of defender through the armpit by aligning wrist to pit

Progression:
Step 1-Depends on the defenders alignment and style. Short lead step or flat step targeted at the playside foot.

Step 2-Quick step down and up into defender, using the shoulder and flipper of the arm opposite playside targeted at the playside number to armpit, while keeping the outside arm free utilizing it for leverage. The opposite applies if playside is away. Flipper technique varies for more aggressive defenders; the near playside arm is applied to the outside shoulder. This allows more force while locking the defender into a fit (fist to point).

Step 3- Continue drive staying square with a great base and body position while eyeing level 2 and forcing the lift of the defenders shoulder. When pushed off block flowing linebacker negating cross face pursuit.

Note: It's imperative to keeps hips and body strong during the progression thus allowing the uncovered to fit and drive. If away from call side and when zone blocking; faced with an outside shade and in no combo with Guard the Tackle will then use this technique to get to level 2 (half-rip).

Drills: Sled, bags.

Pass Protection

Philosophy

Pass protection carries a similar yet different attitude than when run blocking. It should be approached with the same demeanor in terms of technical approach and intensity, but played with steadied patience. When understanding your Line Awareness Points you'll effectively utilize body position, reference points, and counter points before contact is ever made.

Fundamentals of Pass Protection

a. Understand your scheme, approach and desired goal of the play.
b. Utilize Line Awareness. (Explained later.)
c. Know your vulnerable points-if help is coming then where from?
d. Maintain excellent demeanor, a balanced stance and steadied rock.
e. Maintain perfect position and progression while carrying out assignment.
f. Know your opponent's strengths and weaknesses (scouting reports, film study, and development during game).
g. Look for pre-snap technical flaws or indicators by the defender that can alert to stunts, blitzes, moves, and drop-backs. Call what you see!
h. Understand that his first move will be his best, have prepared counters for his moves; look to negate this by changing technique as well as approach (play games).
i. What is the likely transition of the block? Line Awareness.
j. Have a great set, punch (jam), and transition to finish.
k. Move appropriately Power Down–Kick-Slide and in-relation.

At the L.O.S

Split-Base rule is two-three foot split. Splits adjusted by design of the play or technical advantage. Guards will align their toes of their inside foot to heels of the Center (will vary.) Tackles will align evenly with the Guards. Tight end will follow play-side Tackle. This positioning too will be used to our advantage. Good splits create vision lanes along with forcing the defense to cheat pre-snap or run further post-snap. Therefore enabling a smoother transition for stunt or blitz pick up.

Stance-
3pt-Should never be comfortable, however, it will be balanced with the feet closer to parallel and slightly wider than the shoulders; toes forward and weight distributed on the inside or flat area of the feet-especially the inside or power foot. Heels should be on the ground with the ankles flexed and knees over the toes. Hips should be flexed not locked for this is where the base is centered in the hips and buttocks. A strain should be felt in the upper and outer quads. Shoulders

should be square and parallel to the line of scrimmage with the down hand having a slight amount of weight placed on the fingertips. The opposite hand can be clenched and placed outside the knee or cupped over the top of the knee between the thumb and index finger. The move from a 3pt stance to a perfect pass set should be fluent and unimpeded. Eyes forward looking for pre-snap indicators.

Note: Center if faced with a tight shade (1) on either shoulder, keep the near side foot slightly back. This will ensure enough distance for you to snap, set, and get in position with or without help. Remaining techniques will be described in Line Awareness.

2pt- Should never be comfortable, however, it will be balanced with the feet staggered by the inside foot up/outside foot back and slightly wider than the shoulders; toes forward and weight distributed on the inside or flat area of the feet-especially the inside or power foot. Heels should be on the ground with the ankles flexed and knees bent. Hips and buttocks kept low. Hips should be flexed not locked for this is where the base is centered in the hips and buttocks (Rock). A strain should be felt in the upper and outer quads. Shoulders should be square to the line of scrimmage and kept back. Lower back is arched. Hands are placed in one of three positions depending on the player's comfort and position. First, above the thigh pads with the hands open and thumbs slightly over the thigh pad. Second; hands directly over the outside half of the thigh pad with the index finger pointing towards the outside of the knee and thumbs over the pad. Lastly, hands open and placed over and above the kneepads with the thumb inside and index finger outside. Head is kept back with the chin tucked. This keeps your head level. Eyes forward looking for pre-snap indicators.

Notes: Guards stagger is never as deep as the Tackle unless determined by defensive front. Guards, an alternative technique when facing inside/head-up/outside, keep your stagger shallow while placing the elbows over the knees thus lowering your initial base. This is an excellent adjustment versus certain defenders styles. Tackles will narrow their outside knee to ensure transition.

Sets-
Inside-Defender is in an inside shade 1, 2i, 4i, 6i
Head-up-Defender is 0, 2, 4, 6
Outside-Defender is in an outside shade 1(center), 3, 5, 5wide, 9

Punch Points (Jam Technique)-
Pass pro punching is just like when run blocking. You have a target area, which varies depending on defenders alignment but ideally is outside the numbers on the defenders breastplate. Thumbs are facing up; contact is violent and when made a <u>snatch</u> is immediate. Do this by grabbing and squeezing all that your hands can get. It is perfectly legal and when done properly stuns a defender enabling the progression of positioning. Elbows are tight to the body utilizing the strength of

the upper body. Other punch points vary depending on defenders position and his approach. Inside out techniques can be described as Point-pec or Point under. Both are highly effective and add to a lineman's toolbox. In addition a Tackle will employ a one-arm punch if needed (explained later) to separate, bait, or counter a defenders approach.

Note: When contact is imminent hands should be up in front and slightly away from the chest.

Explanation of point: Have 2 players stand in front of each other, one player stand in a good pass pro base with the hands open and parallel to the ground. The other player places his hands over the wrists of the offensive player. On go-have O-player drive his hands up with the defender forcing his hands down. Next, do it again, this time with the offensive player having thumbs up and fist closed. The results are clear thus allowing the show of where the strength and advantage come from. Thumbs up provide much more strength coming from the entire upper body.

Line Awareness Points-Characteristically describes all sets, attack points, and counter actions for an offensive lineman versus defenders in any and all situations.

Line Awareness-
a. What is the scheme?
b. What is my attack point? Where do I need to set, do I have help? Am I helping?
c. Any pre-snap indicators.
d. Potential blitz combo.
e. Always maintain an in-to-out relationship while working to square him up.
f. If inside; G/C, know counters based on defenders rush in relation to where he is now and where he wants to go. Knowing the release point initially gives you that; then as the play unfolds he'll essentially tell you where it is. At what point will he need to reverse direction or change course. 3yd rule (DZ).
g. If outside; Tackles/TE, know counters based on defenders rush in relation to where he is now and where he wants to go. Knowing the release point initially gives you that; then as the play unfolds he'll essentially tell you where it is. At what point will he need to reverse direction or change course.
h. Utilize your toolbox.
i. If inside, Guards, big dual steps (vs. zone blitz) are done by leading with the inside foot first; Tackles lead with the outside foot first. All steps are straight back and need to set the lineman in a perfect pass-pro demeanor with the inside foot up. Guards usually take 2 steps while Tackles take 3. Eyes on nearest defender to near backer. If facing a 3-man line (Guards), kick is the same but slightly out.

Explanation of Point: On a L.O.S-Center & Guards-With normal splits taken spread arms out wide to point out initial area of protection regardless of scheme.

This establishes all that is in front and slightly outside or inside. Tackles-with normal splits taken have a different initial area. Right Tackle points his inside arm at a reference point of 12 on a clock. His outside arm points back to 5 on a clock. The Left Tackle does the opposite, inside to 12 with the outside to 7. Their area of concern unless dictated by scheme is all between those two points of reference.

Versus Head-up-Pick up and put the inside foot slightly to the inside. Look to establish an in to out relationship while squaring him up. Punch and snatch the attack point. Move accordingly keeping the inside foot (common leg) up. Center should pick up the foot away from help if it's coming. If no help then quickly pick up and put down the foot nearest the defender. Get the opposite snap hand up and punch immediately follow through working excellent pass-pro demeanor.

Note: Interior linemen stay big and stay square. Never allow that inside foot to drop step, this opens the hips and allows a defender an inside lane, thus collapsing the pocket.

Versus Inside Shade-Pick up and place the inside foot (power down) inside or as close to his inside foot as possible with the toes pointing forward. Look to square him up. Your Line Awareness automatically tells you that a greater area to protect is outside even though the defender is inside. You have a smaller area inside than outside just by body position alone. Keep in mind your vulnerable points. As you step inside align your inside eye to the defenders outside eye. Deliver a violent punch then snatch while working and maintaining an excellent pass-pro demeanor. Inside leg stays high; anticipate the defender to work outside, by which is automatically covered by your eye alignment and body position. If the defender continues to work inside, power down while working proper demeanor and line awareness. * Mix technique by utilizing a Power Absorb (Softer point-pec) to sumo.

Center-When faced with a 1 technique to either side will have that foot initially set back with the opposite foot slightly up. Unless help is coming will step with the nearest foot out to square up. This step and instant punch with the opposite hand (to snap) will give the Center enough space to transition. Work in to out to square. Utilize Point-Pec or Point Under to snatch. When faced with a defender head-up, pick up and put down the up foot first unless help is coming.

Guard uncovered with Center covered to his side-Take the same steps as versus an inside shade. However, keep the outside arm free while punching the defenders near attack point. Guard cannot snatch technique unless the Nose works to him. Keep eyes up looking for a stunt to blitz by level 2. Keep shoulders square and maintain an excellent pass-pro demeanor.

Center uncovered with Guard covered to his side-Same steps and technical approach as above yet working out instead of in. Pick up and place the near foot (power down) outside or as close to his inside foot as possible with the toes pointing forward. Attacking is never going forward but rather a short kick step laterally or diagonally depending on the defenders style. The attack point is the breastplate of the inside number. Look to square him up. Center cannot snatch technique unless the Nose works to him. Keep eyes up looking for a stunt to blitz by level 2. Keep shoulders square and maintain an excellent pass-pro demeanor.

Versus Outside Shade-

Guards-Versus a 3 technique will always attack. Attacking is never going forward but rather a short kick step laterally or diagonally depending on the defenders style. The attack point is the breastplate of the outside number. Look to square him up. Your Line Awareness automatically tells you that a greater area to protect is inside even though the defender is outside. You have a smaller area outside than inside <u>just by body position alone</u>. Keep in mind your vulnerable points. As you step outside align your outside eye to the middle of the defenders facemask. Deliver a violent punch then snatch while working and maintaining an excellent pass-pro demeanor. Inside leg stays high; anticipate the defender to work inside, by which is automatically covered by your eye alignment and body position. If the defender continues to work outside, kick slide while working proper demeanor and line awareness. * Mix technique by utilizing a Power Absorb to sumo.

Note: Power absorbing is a hard punch with the near fist, while gliding to absorb with the opposite (Point-pec.)

Tackles-Will always step with their outside foot first. However, it depends on the defenders alignment (As stated when inside or head-up step inside first). The closer he is the shorter the step needed laterally or diagonally. Attack point is the breastplate of the outside number. Look to square him up through an in-to-out relationship. Your Line Awareness is different and adjusts by his pre-snap alignment, approach, and style. Upon contact always work with an excellent pass-pro demeanor and line awareness. In an obvious situation or if the Tackle is in a 2pt stance the staggered stance should be slightly wider but based upon the players comfort and technique. It should get you to where you need to be in a perfect pass-pro demeanor. If necessary, initial position can adjust slightly in relation to the guard. (Line-Awareness set-up.)

Line Awareness Point-Tackles will have three recognition points for Ends. Angle A, B, or C. Pre-snap alignments are 4I, 4, 5, wide 5, and 9. Each alignment carries an initial recognition point as well as Tackles approach, counter, and attack point.

Angle A-Ends approach to the Quarterback is in towards the B gap or through the Tackle by his inside or inside number; essentially through him and declared immediately.

Angle B-Ends approach to the Quarterback is usually 2-3 steps up field while transiting the hips and body for a deeper and direct path. This approach gives an End options to his initial outside approach. He now can react to his setup of you.

Angle C-Pure Speed rush; Ends approach to the Quarterback is always outside and wide. Tackles will have a read of the defender for this recognition point, chest or shoulder. (Counter described later.)

From either alignment the defender can approach the three ways, however, what needs to be understood is what the defenders is more likely to do. The closer he is the flatter the kick and more concern for an inside approach. As stated before, utilizing body position will create a lag point (bubble), by which the defender must contend with. Understand that a defender doesn't want to contend with you but rather get by as quickly as possible. Essentially the more bubbles you create the better or easier your block becomes.

4I, 4 technique-Ends have the option of A, B, C. unless by design you'll primarily face A and B recognition points. (Pre-snap indication-Blitz.)

5 technique-Ends have the option of all three-approach points A, B, C. unless by design you'll primarily face B and C recognition points.

5 wide-Ends have the option of all three approach points A, B, C. same as above.

Ghost 9-Ends approach is to beat you outside and right away by speed or quick move outside. In addition, look for the defender to set you up for an inside move.

Tackles approach versus-

<u>5 technique</u>-Slight kick outside flat but diagonal. Hands need to be up ready for contact immediately. Attack point as stated is the breastplate of the outside number. If the defender gives an angle A recognition, return to where you started, punch and keep powering down. Any other approach by the defender, work in to out to square.

<u>5 wide</u>-2 kick steps diagonally will put the tackle in a perfect position (to read the defenders approach) while the hands up are ready to punch. Attack point and

pass- pro finish are the same. *Alternative technique is to power absorb. When reading hands are to be low and aligned just outside and under the ribcage. Path to punch is low to high fit.

<u>Ghost 9</u>-This approach for a tackle is different. In an obvious situation the feet are slightly further apart; enough to give the Tackles an impressive first step while still in a good demeanor. The progression steps are all done by moving in relation

(one foot moves a certain amount the other moves the same) and on the clock points of 5 or 7. Weight should be balanced but slightly placed on the inside. Inside foot will always remain high and grounded while the kick foot will have a slight elevation until such time that contact is made<u>. Be sure to keep the knee of the outside leg pointing forward pre-snap and post-snap or until contact is made. This ensures a smoother kick thus negating hips to lock.</u> Inside arm will remain up and ready to punch by the inside number. The outside arm is used in three-ways, first, for balance and leverage to get the body out and in position, second to punch, and lastly to create an edge for the defender to contend with. Technique for the outside arm is; from the get off keep it locked where it is but away from the body. On the kick slide use this arm by one of two ways, cranking the elbow back or keeping the elbow locked and cranking the fist. The read for a Tackle on defender in this situation is **chest** or **shoulder,** by which if he has chest, attack by punching and locking on (Snatch). When faced with a shoulder read (pure speed rush), kick to the point in to out using your outside arm to create an edge. By doing this, the defender has to contend with it thus allowing you to hop the horse. **Hoping the horse** is a technical term for when a Tackle transitions himself to the inside half of the defender and is now in position to drive to 5 or 7. If you are not in position to attack but have an excellent base then you can easily punch to create space and allow yourself time to regroup. If the defender pulls up and tries to contend with your outside arm then you have several options. Employing this technique has major advantages; a defender might want to rip under it giving the Tackle a rip counter or allowing for additional techniques, such as one-arm punch and bait. *Utilize the power absorb technique versus a shoulder read.

Note: Each offensive lineman based on his Line Awareness has an initial counter to contend for. This as stated earlier is in conjunction with pre-snap indicators, defender style, and scouting report.

LINE-AWARENESS RECOGNITION

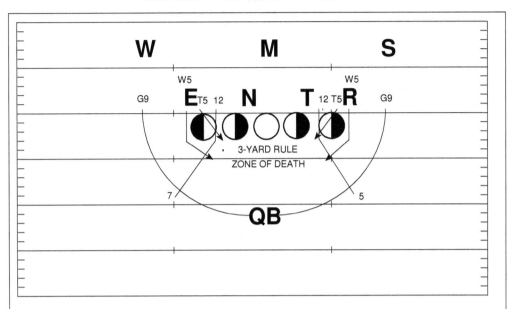

Line Awareness Point -Tackles will will have three recognition points for Ends. Angle A, B, or C. Pre-snap alignments are 4I, 4, 5, wide 5, and 9. Each alignment carries an intial recognition point as well as Tackles approach, attack point, and counter.

Angle A (T5) - Ends approach to the Quarterback is in towards the B gap or through the Tackle by his inside or inside number; essentially through him and declared immediately.

Angle B (W5) - Ends approach to the Quarterback is usually 2-3 steps up field while transiting the hips and body for a deeper and direct path. This approach gives an End options to his initial outside approach. He now can react to his setup of you.

Angle C (G9) - Pure Speed rush; Ends approach to the Quarterback is always outside and wide. Tackles will have a read of the defender for this recognition point, chest or shoulder.

4I, 4 technique - Ends have the option of A, B, C. unless by design you'll primarily face A and B recognition points. (Pre-snap indication-Blitz.)

5 technique - Ends have the option of all three-approach points A, B, C. unless by design, you'll primarily face B and C recognition points.

5 wide - Ends have the option of all three approach points A, B, C. same as above.

Ghost 9 - Ends approach is to beat you outside and right away by speed or quick move outside. In addition, look for the defender to set you up for an inside move.

LINE-AWARENESS RECOGNITION

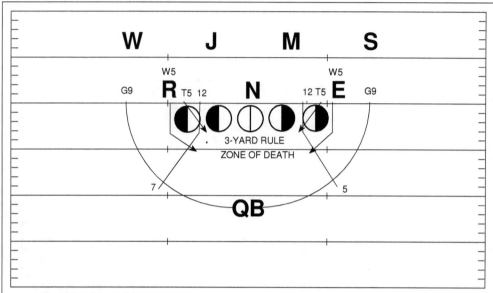

Line Awareness Point -Tackles will will have three recognition points for Ends. Angle A, B, or C. Pre-snap alignments are 4I, 4, 5, wide 5, and 9. Each alignment carries an intial recognition point as well as Tackles approach, attack point, and counter.

Angle A (T5) - Ends approach to the Quarterback is in towards the B gap or through the Tackle by his inside or inside number; essentially through him and declared immediately.

Angle B (W5) - Ends approach to the Quarterback is usually 2-3 steps up field while transiting the hips and body for a deeper and direct path. This approach gives an End options to his initial outside approach. He now can react to his setup of you.

Angle C (G9) - Pure Speed rush; Ends approach to the Quarterback is always outside and wide. Tackles will have a read of the defender for this recognition point, chest or shoulder.

4I, 4 technique - Ends have the option of A, B, C. unless by design you'll primarily face A and B recognition points. (Pre-snap indication-Blitz.)

5 technique - Ends have the option of all three-approach points A, B, C. unless by design you'll primarily face B and C recognition points.

5 wide - Ends have the option of all three approach points A, B, C. same as above.

Ghost 9 - Ends approach is to beat you outside and right away by speed or quick move outside. In addition, look for the defender to set you up for an inside move.

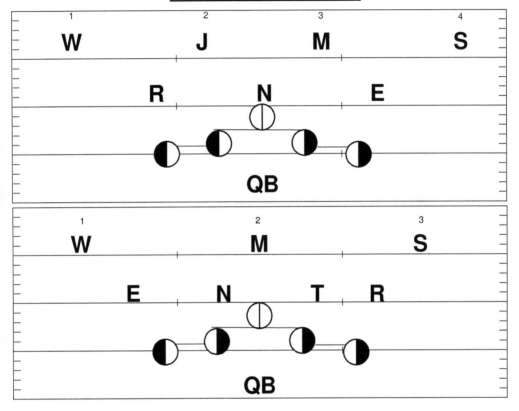

Center on the L.O.S. with a normal stance.
Guards-Align the toes of their inside foot on the heels of the center with a normal split of 2-2+feet while staggering their feet (Stance p.16).
Tackles-With a normal split, will align their toes of their inside foot to slightly above the midfoot (opposite the instep) of the guards outside foot. Stances will be 2pt.

The depth will vary based on the situation (Down & Distance). Shoulders will be square to the L.O.S while the helmet is touching the centers waist-line to ensure a legal set-up. Eyes are immediately aimed at near defender.
*Tackles will have their outside knee narrowed pre-snap while Guards will have a slighter exaggeration in their stagger.

SETS VS. ALIGNMENTS

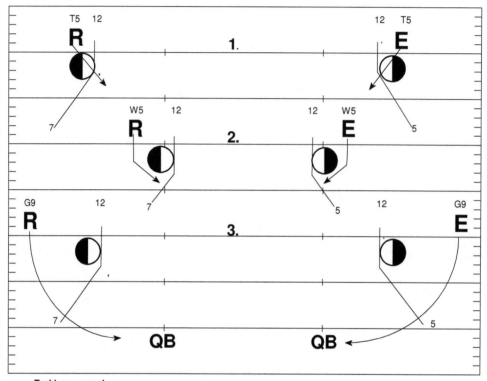

Tackles approach versus-

Row 1 - Angle A (T5) - Ends approach to the Quarterback is in towards the B gap or through the Tackle by his inside or inside number; essentially through him and declared immediately. With this alignment look for his near or inside hand to be down, which can be an indicator for action inside.

<u>5 technique</u> - Slight kick outside (1) flat but diagonal. Hands need to be up up ready for contact immediately. Attack point as stated is the outside breastplate of the outside number. Snatch upon contact. When the defender gives an angle A recognition, return to where you started, punch and keep powering down. Any other approach by defender work in-to-out to square. With this alignment either hand can be down. Usual transition for defender is, left hand down=3 steps while the right=2 steps (can vary.)

Row 2 - Angle B (W5) - Ends approach to the Quarterback is usually 2-3 steps up field while transiting the hips and body for a deeper and direct path. This approach gives an End options to his initial outside approach. He now can react to his setup of you.

<u>5 wide</u> - 2 kick steps diagonally (at 5) will put the tackle in a perfect position (to read the defenders approach) while the hands are up ready to punch. Attack point and pass-pro finish are the same. *Alternative technique here is to power absorb, by which when reading hands are to be low and aligned just outside and under the rib cage. Path to punch is a low to high fit.

Row 3 - Angle C (G9) - Pure Speed rush; Ends approach to the Quarterback is always outside and wide. Tackles will have a read of the defender for this recognition point, chest or shoulder.

Ghost 9 - This approach for a tackle is different. In an obvious situation the feet are slightly further apart; enough to give the Tackles an impressive first step while still in a good demeanor. The progression steps are all done by moving in relation (one foot moves a certain amount the other moves the same) and on the clock points of 5 or 7. Weight should be balanced but slightly placed on the inside. Inside foot will always remain high and grounded while the kick foot will have a slight elevation until such time that contact is made. Be sure to keep the knee of the outside leg pointing forward pre-snap and post-snap or until contact is made. This ensures a smoother kick thus negating hips to lock. Inside arm will remain up and ready to punch by the inside number. The outside arm is used in three-ways, first, for balance and leverage to get the body out and in position, second to punch, and lastly to create an edge for the defender to contend with. Technique for the outside arm is; from the get off keep it locked where it is but away from the body. On the kick slide use this arm by one of two ways, cranking the elbow back or keeping the elbow locked and cranking the fist. The read for a Tackle on defender in this situation is chest or shoulder, by which if he has chest, attack by punching and locking on (Snatch). When faced with a shoulder read (pure speed rush), kick to the point in to out using your outside arm to create an edge. By doing this, the defender has to contend with it thus allowing you to hop the horse. Hoping the horse is a technical term for when a Tackle transitions himself to the inside half of the defender and is now in position to drive to 5 or 7. If you are not in position to attack but have an excellent base then you can easily punch to create space and allow yourself time to regroup. If the defender pulls up and tries to contend with it your outside arm then you have several options. Employing this technique has major advantages; a defender might want to rip under it giving the Tackle a rip counter or allowing for additional techniques, such as one-arm punch and bait.
*Utilize the power absorb technique versus a shoulder read.

As stated above unless an obvious blitz situation the defender will usually set with his outside hand down.

Line Awareness Drill Set-up-
Keys:
Integrity of the drill
Stay disciplined to technique from stance to start to finish
Footwork movements in relation-Power-down-Kick slide. Same amount of space covered.
Switch sides and utilize reference points on the field and towards the defender
High impact with intensity and feet move in relation

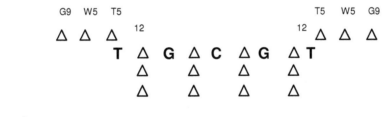

This drill is designed to condition each player how to defend his pass rush lane while simultaneously reacting to how a defender will approach and adjust in relation to where the QB is. Essentially the defender will tell the lineman where the QB is at.
On whistle Guards and Center will power-down and kick slide to each level of the cone which is placed at 1 yard apart. Tackles will set to each cone by kick sliding before powering down. The outside and behind cones are set up at 7x7 deep and back to establish a peripheal point for when the QB will be directly behind or even with the tackle. They are reference points for the tackle to understand that he'll hop the horse and drive, continue to push defender downfield, or be alert for the defender to redirect and comeback inside either by a spin or club under.

SETS VS. ALIGNMENTS (VISUAL)

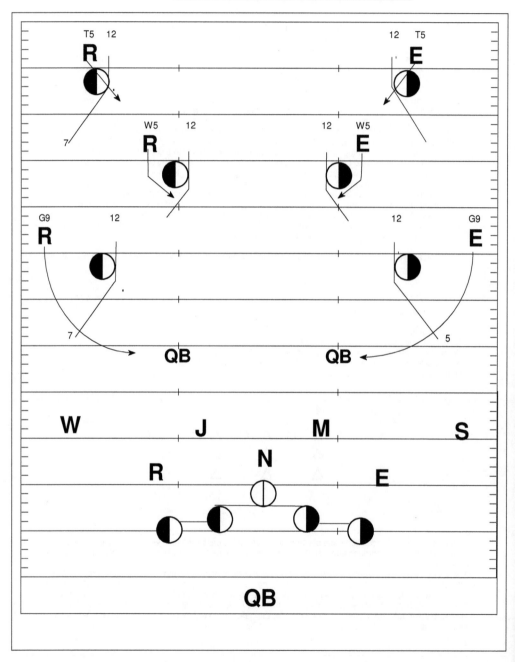

THREE MAN RULES

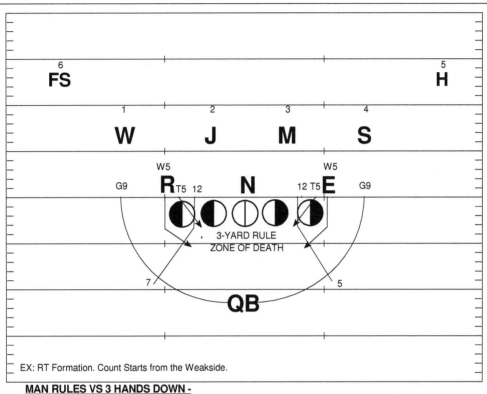

EX: RT Formation. Count Starts from the Weakside.

MAN RULES VS 3 HANDS DOWN -
These rules serve as our base reads when facing any situation that has three hands down with Man protection.
Key Points: 1-Eyes follow threat. 2-Backers feet dictate action.
3-ILB moves outside DE then "Gout" call is made. Potential Fan (Franky) or Man call.

*2 ways of approach. If interior pressure is suspected than "Alert" call is made; Guards will step to the Nose utilizing indicators eying their keys. No alert, than Guards Big Dual steps. Reading in-out.

Versus Alert call:
PST locks on DE and listens.
PSG steps to the Nose. His eyes immediately go to the Mike-Jack-Sam (Removed by form).
PSG sets-reads #3LB. Eyes follow #3. utilizing indicators to feel pressure and upon a visual of LB's intentions; Guard will combo switch unless a "Lock" call is made pre-snap or "Man" call is made post-snap.
Versus 4 hands down, "Push" call comes from C then a Man switch is made from in to out. An obvious Blitz situation with 4 to a side.
C sets and locks on the Nose. Nose away; C locks and listens. Nose Bails; C big duals closest threat.
BSG steps to the Nose. His eyes immediately go the Jack-Mike-Will (Removed by form.) BSG sets-reads # 2. Eyes follow #2. Response is same as PSG.
BST locks on DE and listens.
**If DE Bails (Zone Blitz) read becomes auto BIG Dual. Normal reads take immediate threat in to out. No Pressure, find work.

THREE MAN KEY READS

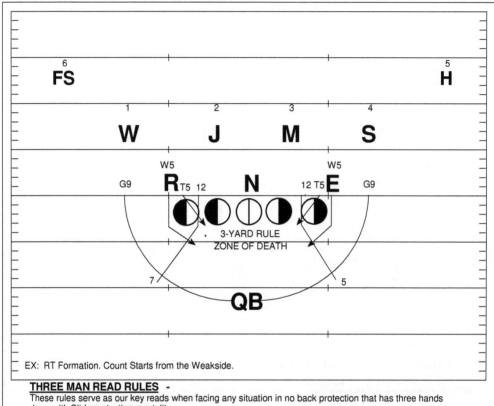

EX: RT Formation. Count Starts from the Weakside.

THREE MAN READ RULES -
These rules serve as our key reads when facing any situation in no back protection that has three hands down with <u>Slide</u> protection mentality.
Key Points: 1-Eyes follow threat.
            2-Backers feet and hips dictate action. Hips are low he is out, hips are high he is coming.

If Play called has a Strong RT formation w/ 5 Man <u>Slide Protection Mentality:</u> Opposite applies if read is from the left.
PST locks on DE.
PSG steps to the Nose utilizing indicators eying the Mike (#3). N is away his eyes immediately go to the Jack-Mike-Sam (Removed by form).
If Nose to; PSG engages and Locks. Versus 4 hands down, "Push" call comes from C then a Man switch is made from in to out. An obvious Blitz situation with 4 to a side.
C steps away from PST and reads Nose-Jack. Nose to; C locks and listens.
Nose is away; C sets firmly and listens while he eyes the Jack-Mike.
BSG steps to the DE. DE is away his eyes immediately go the Will-Jack-Mike. If Will (1) vacates and FS (6) shows he becomes primary threat unless backer is first.
DE attacks A Gap (Stick Tech). BSG Locks on DE, while BST slides off and reads Will-Free-Jack.
BST kicks out based on L.A. DE to, he locks. DE away his eyes go to the Will-Free-Jack.
****If DE Bails (Zone Blitz) read becomes auto BIG Dual. Normal reads take immediate threat in to out. No Pressure, potential "<u>Alamo</u>" call. Sift and find work usually opposite side threat A-B-C-D gap.

Sprint Out Pass-Protection

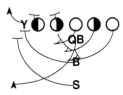

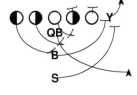

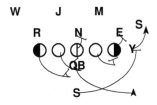

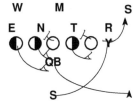

Examples of Sprint Out protection

Sprint out protection is designed to move the pocket while simultaneously maintaining protection.

The protection varies on the front, alignment of defenders, and scheme of the play.

A lineman who is covered to the call side will set to reach and follow with normal run progression techniques to get to the point of attack. At the P.O.A. the setting lineman will transition his feet to place his outside foot in the up position and inside foot back. His objective is to maintain the edge while inviting and forcing action to the inside. The uncovered lineman to the call side will set (can vary) up behind the setting lineman by taking a deeper and exaggerated bucket to establish an area of protection with his outside foot up and inside foot back (transition). This puts him in an opposite sided stance with a power down progression until contact is made. The goal is to maintain a forward seal and force action inside.

An uncovered lineman will set based on the front, and alignment of defender in/on/ or near him. A slide open stab technique will align the setting lineman on the inside hip of his partner to the call side, while eying his target area and action of the defense. His objective is to seal and maintain the inside while forcing action to his outside and away from the roll. The pocket will keep moving until such time that the area has been reached and that contact is imminent and firm.

Keys: It's imperative to utilize communication, indicators, technique, and the transition of the feet.

Drills:
Step to set 1/2/3 utilizing indicators Go-2-go, Static steps
Cones.

Slide Protection

Examples of Slide Protection

Slide Protection is used in a number of ways and is an excellent protection versus a blitz situation where the defense brings 4 to a side or a blitz combo by defenders travels more than 2 gaps. It places offensive lineman in an area by which, facilitates reads and reaction.

Slide progression from the right. Depends on the scheme and front of the defense. The slide usually will start by the first uncovered or first setting offensive lineman (will vary). If called the other way the opposite applies.

If covered the first step is to power down 1-2 steps while eying and keying your defender in/on/ or near your slide path. Upon first step and no imminent contact, 1 more step is needed before transitioning feet to an inverded stagger. Steps are for width without going to deep. If contact is made then square up and follow through with a normal pass-pro finish.

Keys: It's imperative to utilize communication, line awareness, indicators, as well as target areas during the slide.

Steps-Depends on the front, alignment of defender, and direction of the slide.

<u>Away from call side and in slide-</u>
Leading with the inside foot (upfoot). Set normally as you would versus an inside shade for 1-2 steps before transitioning feet to a kick-slide progression. Covered (if not solid)-same applies if contact is not made while eying target area. If contact is made finish is normal.

<u>At the call side-</u>
Set normally as you would versus an outside shade, keying near defender to target area. Response is based upon contact, place in slide, and action of defender.

Drills: Step to set 1/2/3 utilizing indicators Go-2-go, Static steps, and Cones.

Tight Ends in Pass Protection-

Tight Ends will follow all Line Awareness points of a Tackle as stated above. When setting to a wide defender (OLB/CB) from a pre-snap indicator that is a man removed will kick straight back (starting with the outside foot first). If his approach tightens pre-snap then set and attack as a Tackle would in that situation.

Pass Protection Points

a. Know your scheme and goal of the play.
b. Communicate pre-snap indicators, call what you see, talk to your partner.
c. Have and maintain excellent demeanor.
d. Move swiftly and accordingly (in relation), (Power Down-Kick Slide).
e. Be patient time your punch and snatch.
f. Work to and maintain in to out to square up relationship (Sumo if necessary).
g. Know your Line Awareness.
h. Utilize counters and entire toolbox.
i. If uncovered or untested, never stand idle; find work and explode into defender within the scheme.
j. Don't ever stop pass blocking.
k. Change approach, play games and negate his best move.
l. When you see the ball thrown, get downfield and continue blocking.

Common Faults in Pass Protection
a. Miss-communication, pre-snap and post-snap.
b. Poor stance, set, and punch, eyes closed at point of attack.
c. Poor pass-pro-demeanor.
d. Giving the defender leverage before and after contact.
e. Too aggressive/leaning.
f. Too passive/on heels.
g. Weak punch (jam) and lock.
h. Poor transition of demeanor (Power down/Kick slide).
i. Over setting.
j. Dropping inside leg (opening the door).
k. Locking hips.
l. Failing to Sumo for hand positioning or recover to regroup.

Counters-

Are essential tools for an offensive lineman to contend against defenders ability to strike a move while pass rushing. Defenders usually will employ their best moves first and second. However, defenders do work to set up linemen for a specific move. In addition, defenders do have counters to our counters so goes the transition.

Common Transitions

a. Rip outside to spin inside.
b. Rip outside to jump swim outside.
c. Rip outside to jump club inside.
d. Opposite inside to outside for above rip moves.
e. Swim outside to rip outside.
f. Swim outside to rip outside to spin inside.
g. Opposite inside to outside for above swim moves.
h. Bull rush.
i. Bull rush wide to a rip inside.
j. Push to pull, used with swim either way or wash technique.
k. Club outside with swim or rip.
l. Club inside with swim or rip.
m. Double club either way.

Note: Be alert for stutter steps, head fakes and spin at P.O.A.

Counter Tools-<u>All explanations will be versus outside moves</u>. Apply the opposite techniques versus inside moves while transitioning the body accordingly. Line Awareness point, after initial counter, look for above transitions and move with progression techniques.

Versus Rip-In perfect pass-pro demeanor and upon punch, outside hand is open and placed between the numbers high on the breastplate aligning the neck between the index finger and thumb. The inside hand is punched down and screwed into the defenders inside hip fitting it between the index finger and thumb. Align hip to hip and drive the inside hand down while pushing back on the upper chest. *If separation exists between the hips, this counter will not work. If this occurs, just punch-off and reset.

Result: When done properly the defender should snap.

Versus Swim- In perfect pass-pro demeanor and upon punch, outside hand is open and in position to punch, glide, or snatch. Inside hand is open and punched at the inside shoulder. After punching, sumo for perfect position.

Result: Swim shoulder should snap back thus forcing defender to secondary move.

Versus Bull- In perfect pass-pro demeanor and upon punch, two-ways to counter a Bull rush. First, jump technique; do this by lateral stepping (Flat progression) towards the defender utilizing a violent punch and helmet placement (similar to a head butt). Get tight and work progression. The second counter is to hop back (Anchor) and regroup working excellent pass-demeanor.

Result: First technique; defender is stunned, stalemated then forced to secondary move. Second, defender loses momentum then forced to counter. If you feel the rip, it would be better to lock and drive then immediately shifting to a rip counter.

Versus Push-Pull- In perfect pass-pro demeanor and upon punch with snatch, utilize a steady rock by pressure versus the push while sitting versus the pull. It is imperative to maintain a wide base and fluent movement. Look and feel for transitions explained above; respond accordingly.

Result: Defender loses against a great base thus forcing secondary move.

Versus Club- Guards/Center-In perfect pass-pro demeanor and upon punch with snatch; Lock out keeping perfect pass-pro demeanor while moving laterally to the club side. Don't overstep or lose L.A. Look and feel for transitions explained above; respond accordingly. *Utilize a glide (power absorb) for inside control.

Tackles-In perfect pass-pro demeanor and upon punch, when defenders chest is close enough snatch and lock-on following through with progression. If it's telegraphed and done from a wide rush then look to One-Arm Judo Punch. Do this by blocking the club with the outside forearm while simultaneously punching with the inside arm at the defenders nearest shoulder or attack point. Follow through with progression maintaining excellent demeanor and L.A. At the very least it will allow the Tackle to jam and regroup.
If attempted inside, the Tackle will punch, snatch while powering down and driving vertically.

Result: Guards/Center; this keeps defender inside and square. Tackles; forces the secondary move with defender losing leverage and power. Lastly, it plays into our strengths of squaring him up.

Tools for the Tool Box in Pass Protection

Point Pec/Point under-Depending on the lineman's position; worked from inside out or Outside in. From inside; inside arm attacks defenders near shoulder while the outside arm snatches outside defenders outside (Pec) breastplate. Point under has the same approach, however, this time the outside arm snatches under the breastplate of the outside number. Work to square and follow through with progression. From outside; reverse the techniques but maintain the same finish.

Bait technique-Several ways to employ this technique. Upon set, throw hands out and in punch position until such time that the defender will contend with them. When he does pull back and punch to snatch. The other way is by baiting the nearest shoulder towards the defender. Follow through with finish or transition.

Head Butt-From an excellent set and demeanor; punch, snatch and utilize the area just above your facemask on your helmet. Work to finish. Do not wind up or lunge. It should be quick and used with enough force to stun the defender.

Butt Block-Excellent recovery if spun around or position is lost during pass-pro. Keep hips low and drive buttocks into defender while locking arms back thus keeping the defender shelled into your body. At this point block till the whistle.

Recovery-If pass-pro positioning is lost then pivot off the foot to the side that you are losing. Recover towards the opposite direction and look to cut. If losing but not quite lost and still having in to out positioning then align hip to hip and drive hip into defender. If possible sumo to recover.

Cut Block-Used by various schemes. Be sure to set it up and when used effectively will take the defender off his rush and hands out of the pass lane. In addition it will slow a defender down.

Draw Technique-Has 2 methods to be employed. First, bait by setting to the side towards the draw. Do not over-exaggerate this step make it impressive to sell. When the defender is close enough, plant and club with the fist to the draw side targeted at his near tricep thus forcing the defender away from the draw. The second technique is a pure outside sell versus an outside alignment; maintain in to out position and when the defender is close enough wash (punch) with both hands at his inside tricep thus forcing him away from the draw outside.

Blocking Line Stunts-
Description: Combo cross of 2 or more defenders.
Penetrator-is first defender to attack the called gap through the man.
Looper-is second defender who steps back and attacks behind and to the area vacated by the penetrator.

Note: When faced with more than two defenders in a stunt the offensive players will combo respond based on the protection called and necessity of the slide.

Common terminology:

Tan-Tackle first, Nose second.
Nat-Nose first, Tackle second.
Edge-End first, Tackle second.
Tex-Tackle first, End second.
Bex-Backer first, End second

Progression:
2 man set versus an Edge Stunt: All set ups and approaches will be the same based on the defenders alignment. Tackle sets and based on L.A will have an (A) recognition (Penetrator). This automatically has him powering down. The Guard

sets to his L.A point and sees his man is (Looping) vacating out and away. With an established base the Guard will immediately point his eyes in the direction the looper is headed. Upon seeing the defender attacking, he'll set just behind the inside shoulder of the Tackle and with an excellent demeanor attack and slam the penetrator while calling "Switch". This alerts the Tackle that he now in a stunt combo and upon a visual will punch off slide out and attack the looper. *The Guard will align his inside eye to the defenders outside cheek prior to contact.

2 man set versus a Tex Stunt: All set ups and approaches will be the same based on the defenders alignment. The exact opposite occurs; the Tackle will set behind the outside shoulder of the Guard in an excellent pass-pro demeanor. Eyeing the looper will take him right to the penetrator. Upon attacking and slamming the defender he'll call out "Switch", alerting the Guard that he is now in a stunt combo and upon a visual will slide out (in) punch off and attack the looper.

Notes: Regardless of stunt, the setting offensive linemen will always maintain an excellent base with the inside foot up while working to keep shoulders square. If unable to "Switch" then a "Man" call will alert your partner that a stunt is on but a switch can not be made. Unless the Center is involved always set and attack with the assumption that no stunt is on. The transition should be solid and smooth; do this by not allowing a seam to develop. Upon a pass off or "switch call" be sure to get an effective punch off thus allowing an easier transition under the block. If the Center is involved with both Guards and no other responsibility draws him away; then he'll set to his assignment side and respond accordingly. This can be done by one of two ways. First, if congestion occurs then the Center can simply take a glide step back and respond accordingly. Second; upon setting redirect and recover base by stepping back with the first step taken and slightly kicking back the opposite foot thus allowing the repositioning of the up and back foot. This effectively keeps his area big and occupied. *Defenders have a tendency to show their intentions, so call what you see. When applicable utilize a reverse rip of the penetrator to get square.

Versus Down player and Backer:
If down defender and backer are in your combo then utilize the same techniques and demeanor as above.

If Backer is "Humming" and cheating the 3 or 4I then, "Bex" call is made by the Guard; this alerts your partner that stunt could be on with near Backer and DE. This situation the Guard sets the Backer as a 3Technique while Tackle sets strait back with his inside foot high slightly behind the level of the Guard in an excellent pass-pro demeanor; eyeing the DE utilizing indicators to read ½ Backer. Upon the Guard setting to attack the LB, and depending on the defenders alignment; if the Backer attacks; the Tackle will set and rip (Steer) the backer away from the inside while calling out "Switch". The Guard now knows that he is in a stunt combo, and will keep his L.A point; not to get over extended; therefore eying the penetrator will take him right to the looper, only squaring up after the

LB commits. Upon the "Switch" call and a visual he'll punch off slide out (in) and square up the DE.

Notes: With this particular stunt the DE will either hesitate or take 2 vertical steps up field before looping. At times, it can be felt before seen, by a slighter (passive) get-off than normal.

Pure attack from a blitzing backer or safety inside:
Set normally and in an excellent demeanor when the LB/S is close enough lower hips and uncoil into him with a violent punch while keeping shoulders square (stay big) to maintain leverage. Keep eyes open at all times.

Note: Footwork is the key. On approach align yourself in his blitz path, maintaining in-to-out leverage. Do not lean or lunge or prematurely anticipate contact. Time the jam and post with the nearest foot. If inside the gap-inside foot, while outside the gap-outside foot.

Tight End

Tight End Releases-
Five Points-
1. Rip out-Slight bucket step with the outside foot while dropping the inside shoulder and ripping up and across the defenders chest.
2. Swim out-Depends on defenders alignment and pattern called; T-board or Flat step towards the playside while the opposite arm is quickly shot up and over the defender.
3. Rip or swim w/club or wash (slap)-Same as above, but utilizing the playside arm to disengage.
4. Block release (Punch Out)-Depends on defenders alignment; T-board or Flat step. Attack defender with the near shoulder while keeping your head to the side of the release.
5. Arc release-Used for pass release or wide release to block 2nd or 3rd level when defender is head-up to inside. Bucket step with the outside foot to get separation. Finish normally.

PAT-FIELD GOAL

When on the L.O.S:

When on the line and from the snapper out:
   a. Guards-Inside toe aligns with the snapper's midfoot. Slight stagger with inside foot back.
   b. Tackles-Inside foot aligns evenly with Guards outside foot. Slight stagger with inside foot back.
   c. Tight Ends-Inside foot aligns evenly with Tackles outside foot. Slight stagger with inside foot back.
   d. Wings-off of the L.O.S with shoulders and body angled at 45° setting just behind the outside foot of the TE's. Inside foot is pointed at the heel of the Tight Ends outside foot.

Note: Splits from the Snapper to the TE's will be approximately 2-3 inches (can vary) or enough to allow for a complete step with the inside foot to the inside of the outside foot of the interior lineman.

Progression:

Guards, Tackles, and Tight Ends stance will be flatfooted while placing a greater emphasis of weight on their outside foot. Body position will be 2pt with a tremendous emphasis of starting and staying low. To do this forearms will be placed over the thigh boards while keeping shoulders square to the line of scrimmage. Fists are clenched and ready to punch. A strain of the upper and outer quads should be felt. Buttocks and hips should be tense and at the maximum height of the squat (can vary). Head up and eyes forward. Upon the snap all linemen between the Wings with the exception of the snapper will step with the inside foot to the inside of the outside foot of the interior lineman. The outside foot will remain cemented to the ground. It is imperative to not allow a crease to develop or to allow that inside foot to lift after it has been planted. The Punch is with both hands (inside/outside gap) but essentially applied to half a man (Gap Down) unless defenders alignment dictates otherwise.

Wings stance will be 2pt with the same technical application as above. To obtain initial position the Wings will use their inside hand by touching the lower back of the Tight End. Upon the snap, Wings will step with their outside foot (opposite the TE) laterally (to themselves) while cementing their inside foot. The step will be just enough to put you in an excellent demeanor ready for contact. The Punch is slightly different but with the same concept. Inside hand will stab and hold inside while the outside hand will punch the inside armpit of the nearest defender (Greatest threat) to the outside.

Note: Tight Ends and Wings in case of a bad snap or "Fire Call", TE will get to the deepest corner (Pylon) near side. The Wing will get over the goal line to the nearest pylon.

Thought: PAT/FG blocking carries a mentality of a 2 second war. Stay big, stay square and protect the inside. You must be 100% here.

DRILLS & SKILLS

        Skills (Pre-practice)..

Blocking Drills
        Firm Roll & Power Strain...
        Climb & Fit-n-Finish..
        Flat Back & Hip Explosion...
        Drive the Bus & steer Technique..
        ½ Man Block & Down/Back Block...
        Cut 1 & 2...
        Crab & Isolation ....
        Cut-off & Twirl ....
        Boards to Backer & Flat-n-Up..
        Acceleration & Zone covered/uncovered..
        Full Line..
        Zone vs. 2 & 3...
        Zone Combos (Half-line)..
        Zone vs. Tags..
        Zone vs. Line Stunts..
        Post 1 & 2..
        Trap & Pulling...
        Fold Blocking & Screen set up...

Pass Protection
        Stance & Power Wave...
        Jam & Jam Set...
        Line Awareness..
        Big Dual...
        Line Awareness set-up...
        Gauntlet..
        Double vs. Pass rusher & Mirror..
        Sumo & One-Arm Shuffle...
        Sailor Shuffle & ¼ punch...
        Ball Punch..
        Down the Line & Push pull..
        Slide..
        Counters...
        Set to blitz & Patience...

Schemes
        Power Drill..
        Scoop-n-climb...

SKILLS

Pre-Practice Drills

Function: To warm up physically and mentally

Set-up:
1. Alternate warm-ups to keep it fresh while working different skills

A. Duck wave-Follow duck wave drill
B. Stance & start, then add drive progression with it
C. Pwer wave-Follow power wave drill
D. Duck walk-From a 2pt squatted stance walk then touch the ground on command or every few steps
E. Board walk-Follow board circuit 2-3 times
F. Hip kicks-Loosen hips by kicking back like a karate kick (perform in between power wave)
G. Texas-2-step-Stagger directly over a line with hands on hips open hips and kick back while staying on the line
H. Screen counts- Walk then progress to full go with screen rules
I. 4-cones-Set up 4 cones 5 yards by 4 yards then duck walk/power down/ power back/ then power down to finish
J. 3-cones-Set up 3 cones to make a right and left triangle, duck walk/ then kick slide/then power down
K. Line awareness-Pass sets and kick slide in set up
L. Hop the horse-Extension of line awarness
M. C-QB exchange-snaps with boards

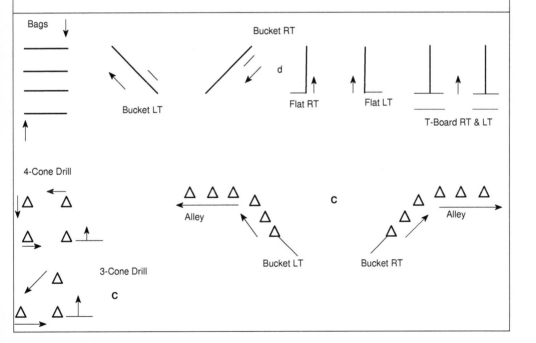

DRILLS

Stance

Function: To properly get into a set position when on the L.O.S.

Set-up:
1. Stack your players to form even or close to groups on a line.
2. On command have the players walk out to form enough groups 5 yds apart vertically by 4 yds horizontally.
3. Start all players in a right stance.
4 a. Set stagger-Toe to instep (can modify) with the inside foot up while toes are pointing slightly outward
   b. Feet align with the shoulders or tighter depending on players height
   c. Roll shoulders back to squeeze blades while flexing chest out
   d. Squat down bringing the chest over the thigh muscles creating the "Z" shape from thigh to foot
   e. With eyes to the sky snap right hand straight out just under chin
   f. Snap it down on the ground with modified wieght applied, fingertips should be flat
   g. Back flat in 3pt, while slightly arched in 2pt

Drill: Can be done by commands or whistle
After setting stagger and upper body-
Commands:
1-snap down
2-hand straight out with eyes to the sky
3-hand down
4-hand up to check for balance
5-hand down
6-freeze and wait to be checked out

Note: If needed have players shake it out and restart thus checking remaining players
Perform both ways.

Duck Wave Drill

Function: To teach walking and driving with leverage and power angles

Set-up: Same as above with all players in a 2pt stance

Drill: Can be done by commands or whistle
After setting stagger and upper body-two ways to completion

A. As a group power walk for 5 yds then walk out 5yds. Turn around and go back.
B. Power walk for 5 yds then walk out 2yds turn around and reset at finish point of 5yds, wait to go back.
C.*Perform forward-backward-and side to side.
Commands:
1. Players power walk (duck demeanor) by stepping and picking up real estate 4-6" while maintaining their stagger driving on the inside halves of their feet
2. At times on command stop and have players check stagger to ensure no overstepping. Quickly restart til finish
3. On command return and go back

Key points:
Maintain excellent power angles
Emphasize pounding the feet into the ground
Control upper body with elbows flexed at 90 degrees with fist going no higher than shoulders or lower than hips
High intensity and high impact is critical.

Steps and Angles of Departures Drill

Function: Departing the L.O.S (T-Board, Flat, Bucket)

Set-up:
1. Set each player 5yds x 5yds.
2. Have every other row take 2 lateral steps, so that each row is staggered for better vision.
3. Each player utilizes boards for proper steps.
4. Start with all players in the same stance RT or LT, then progress to starting by position related.

Board set-up

T-Board ⊥

Flat ⌊ ⌋

Bucket ∨ ∨

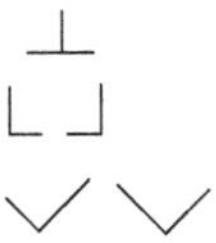

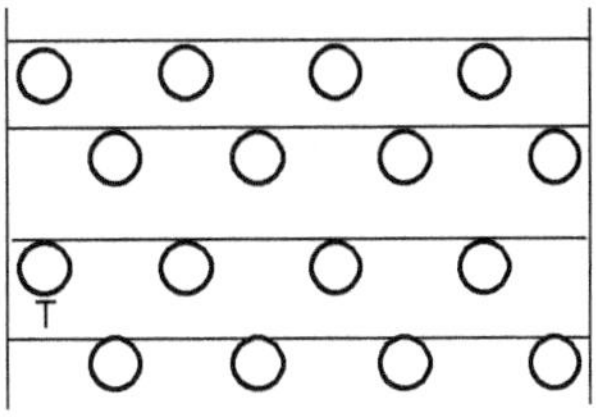

Drill:
On command
1. Go-Step 1 x3
2. Go-2-Step 2x3
3. Go-2-go-Step 3x1
4. Full-go

C

Variations:
Partner with bags
Chute

Perform all steps going one way before moving to the other. When partnered be sure that defender is aligned 2 yds off the ball so as to allow 2 steps to contact. Defender moves on second command.

For T-board-start behind with the vertical board aligned in the middle, so the first step is up and over the board. Keep vertical board aligned in the middle to ensure proper width while driving

For Flat-start with the boards aligned in an L shape RT or LT while the horizontal board is aligned on the heels to prevent a false step while emphasizing that hard quick lateral step.

For Bucket-start with the inner point of the 45 degree board at the nearest foot, so as to allow for depth and alignment on the proper angle.

Firm Roll (Strain)

Function: 3rd step of drive progression when stalemate occurs. Ex: If stepping with the right foot the firm roll will be with the left knee at step 2.

Set-up:
1. Partner up on a line with separation between pairs while the offensive player is facing away
2. Form fit the offensive player into an excellent run demeanor with a designated foot up (stagger)
*Utilize this drill in open space, boxes, or chute

Drill: On command (Full go & controlled)
1-Drop the knee of the upfoot over the toe of the same foot
2-While straining to roll, maintain the block by quickly getting the next step down thus increasing your drive vertically. Strain for 5yds, finishing normally.
3-When at the 5yd mark have partners switch and drive back with the same foot.
4-Restart with the opposite foot up.

Key points:
This drill is done at full speed and in controlled steps
Maintain proper power angles with leverage at all times
Steps should be 4-6", do not overstep while driving on the inside halves of the feet
Intensity and impact along with the proper counter pressure by defender is critical
When block becomes more difficult or stalemate increases then just drop the knee lower over the toes for greater leverage

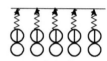

C

Power Strain

Function: Advanced progression of the drill above

Set-up:
1. Place groups of 3 on a line with proper separation while the offensive player is facing away
2. Form fit the offensive player into 2 defenders holding 1or 2 bags in an excellent run demeanor with a designated foot up (stagger)
*Utilize this drill in open space, boxes, or chute

Drill: On command
1-Drop the knee of the upfoot over the toe of the same foot
2-While straining to roll, maintain the block by quickly getting the next step down thus increasing your drive vertically. Strain for 5yds, finishing normally.
3-When at the 5yd mark have partners switch and drive back with the same foot.
4-Restart with the opposite foot up.

Key points:
This drill is done at full speed and in controlled steps
Maintain proper power angles with leverage at all times
Steps should be 4-6", do not overstep while driving on the inside halves of the feet
Intensity and impact along with the proper counter pressure by defenders is critical
When block becomes more difficult or stalemate increases then just drop the knee lower over the toes for greater leverage
Keep the integrity of the drill crisp and clean

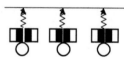

C

Climb

Function: To develop and feel the climb or natural development while run blocking

Set-up:
1. Partner up on a line with normal separation
2. Form fit the offensive player into an excellent run demeanor with a designated foot up (stagger) starting at the defenders waist
*Utilize this drill in open space, boxes, or chute

Drill: On command
1-Full go with progression from start to finish for 5yds.
Drive defender utilizing an excellent fit, firm roll, power angle, flat back, 4-6" steps, wide base, while maintaining balance and leverage
2-When at the 5yds, switch and return
3-Restart with the opposite foot up

Key points:
This drill is done at full speed with high intensity and impact
Pick up real estate by not oversteeping yet driving to to lift defender out of his shoes
this automatically has the lineman working his feet under the defenders
proper counter pressure by defender
Finish with more violence than when started *we never wind down only up*
Finish by punching and pushing as violently as posible (Climb) beat
him up and physically ware him down

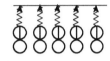

C

Fit-n-Finish

Function: To develop and feel the final phase of a run block when in a proper fit

Set-up:
1. Partner up on a line with normal separation
2. Form fit the offensive player into an excellent run demeanor with a designated foot up (stagger)
*Utilize this drill in open space, boxes, or chute

Drill: On command
1-Full go with progression from start to finish for 5yds.
Drive defender utilizing an excellent fit, firm roll, power angle, flat back, 4-6" steps, wide base, while maintaining balance and leverage
2-When at the 5yds, switch and return
3-Restart with the opposite foot up

Key points:
This drill is done at full speed with high intensity and impact
Pick up real estate by not overstepping yet driving to to lift defender out of his shoes
this automatically has the lineman working his feet under the defenders
proper counter pressure by defender
Finish with more violence than when started *we never wind down only up*
Finish by punching and pushing as violently as posible (Climb) beat
him up and physically ware him down

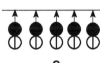

C

Flat-Back

Function: To practice maintaining a Power Angle while keeping an excellent run demeanor

Set-up:
2-ways to perform
A. 1. Partner up on a line with normal separation
2. Form fit the offensive player into an excellent run demeanor with a designated foot up (stagger)
*Utilize this drill in open space, boxes, or chute
B. 1. Place offensive player in a 4pt stance, while his partner places his hands on his shoulders slightly pressing down.
*Utilize this drill in open space, boxes, or chute

Drill: On command
1-Power walk from start to finish for 5yds.
Drive defender utilizing an excellent fit, firm roll, power angle, flat back, 4-6" steps, wide base, while maintaining balance and leverage
2-When at the 5yds, switch and return
3-Restart with the opposite foot up
B. 1-On command from the 4 pt stance begin crawling whith a flat back while trying to climb out without leaving the ground
2. When at the 5yds, switch and return
Key points:
This drill is done at moderate speed with high intensity and impact
Pick up real estate by not oversteping yet driving while maintaining leverage and a power angle
this automatically has the lineman working his feet under the defenders
When done out of a 4pt keep eyes to the sky while holding a flat back with low hips

Hip Explosion

Function: To harness strength and power at the point of attack

Set-up:
1. Align player in front of a bag or sled
2. Player should be in a 6pt (Hands, knees, toes) then progress to a 4pt stance
3. Player should have a flat back, head up, eyes to the sky, strain in the buttocks, tight elbows, and thumbs to the sky

Drill:
1. On command have the palyer fire out and explode into the bag utilizing all the coaching points above while snapping and rolling the hips into the bag
2. Contact should be 3pt contact and when done correctly the player should violently punch and roll out of position while maintaining contact with the bag
3. Drill can be done in reps of three; by exploding out and landing on the belly for 2 reps, then finishing by holding the last one with the hands on the bag

Key points:
This drill can be performed from a 6pt while progressing to a 4 pt
It can be done on a sled, with patners and bags in a chute or open space
This drill is done with high impact and intensity

Drive the Bus

Function: To stay in the run fit while drive blocking

Set-up:
1. Partner up on a line with separation between pairs with the offensive player facing away
2. Form fit the offensive player into an excellent run demeanor with a designated foot up
3. Utilize this drill in open space, in boxes, or from a chute

Drill:
1. On command have the player roll out of the block utilizing all of the proper coaching points taught previously in an excellent run demeanor
2. While driving give a direction that the defender will pull the offensive player in
3. Change directions by pointing RT or LT
4. When at the 10 yd mark have partners switch and return
5. Restart with the opposite foot up

**Progressive drill
1. This drill is set up and completed the same way
2. The difference is that the defender controls the pull and direction
3. It's done with more violence and tempo

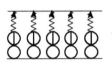
10 yds

Key points:
Maintain an excellent run demeanor
High impact and intensity
Keep balance and leverage
Eyes wide while feeling as well as seeing

C

Steer Technique

Function: To utilize pressure to counter pressure when run blocking against a defender for zone or open field blocking thus facilitating in movement or pancakes

Set-up: (This drill has several variations to it)
1. Partner up on a line with separation between pairs with the offensive player facing away
2. Form fit the offensive player in a bucket (check step) step (OZ) going RT
3. This position should have his inside leg high to simulate his second step
4. Utilize this drill in open space or boxes

Drill:
1. On command have the player step with the next proper step (in this fit, RT) and drive while working for outside leverage while feeling the pressure of the defender
2. At the next command or whistle the defender will fight to not give up outside leverage by placing a greater emphasis with his outside arm by punching or locking out hard
3. This exertion of pressure will be felt by the O-player and when it's felt, the O-player will punch (respond with greater pressure) with his outside arm (baiting the defender) then lock and pull while simultaneously punching up and through with the opposite arm at the inside pec or shoulder
4. This movement should force the defenders shoulders to immediately blade thus facilitating in a pancake or loss of body leverage
5. Have players switch and return with the same foot, complete both ways
6. Work to full progression RT and LT

Key points:
Perform this drill the same way while placing the defender in an unbeatable position thus forcing the lineman to punch hard and through with the inside arm
Work to a full go from a stance to the zone block
Head, face, and body control are a must for this technique to be successful

C

½ Man Block

Function: Used primarily in zone schemes; serves as the base principle for the covered or front side lineman. This is done to maintain play side leverage.

Set-up:
1. Partner up on a line with separation between pairs with the offensive player facing away
2. This drill is done vs. in/on to simulate the different shades when stepping playside
3. Perform this drill in open space, on a line, or in boxes

Drill:
1. On command have the player take a short lead step (T-board) or flat step targeted at the playside foot
2. Normal progression has the player taking a second step with contact, at the P.O.A the lineman will strike the defender using the shoulder and flipper of the arm opposite playside targeted at the playside number to armpit, while keeping the outside arm free utilizing it for leverage or securing the fit.
3. Continue drive staying square with a great base and body position
4. Upon completion of the go-2-go method, reset then go full go
5. Switch players and complete vs. all shades

Key points:
Note: It's imperative to keeps hips and body strong during the progression thus simulating an uncovered to fit and drive.
For a more aggressive block or vs a true double team utilize this block by aligning the near shoulder under the defender's playside #

C

Down/Back Blocks

Function: To block a defender inside or seal an area vacated by a pulling lineman.

Set-up:
1. Partner up on a line or in boxes with the defender offsetting to a designated shade or technique
2. Place a board or object that will cause the player to stress enough to lift and place the near foot up and over it
3. Can be performed with or without bags

Drill:
1. On command have the player fire out utilizing all the proper coaching points to secure the fit while simultaneously picking up real estate
2. Start out with go-2-go, then progress to full go
3. Perform vs. a penetrator (aggressive defender) or looper (swim or spin out) in both directions

Key points:
Proper steps and aiming points
Same demeanor vs aggressive or non-aggressive defender

C

Cut Drill

Function: To cut the legs out from under a defender neutralizing him in his place

Set-up:

2 types of cuts must be worked on
A-Open field
B-On the L.O.S
1. Set up an open area or boxes that covers 5yds by 5yds
2. Pair up and place a defender near a stand up bag to reset the bag after it's cut or utilize pop-ups

Drill: 1
1. On command the player will fire out by taking a bucket step in the designated direction towards the bag
2. The player will adjust, align, and follow through with an excellent cut technique at the P.O.A
3. Upon the cut, the defender will reset the bag and hustle to his starting point and quickly get in the readied position
4. Complete both ways to satisfaction

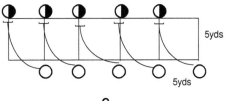

C

Drill: 2

Set-up
1. Create the same set-up with the players in a closer proximity as a down or back block

Drill:
1. On command fire out by taking a bucket step in the designated direction towards the bag
2 For this particular drill a technical variation is to fire out and upon the proper cut fit will crab until the whistle.
3. Complete both ways

Key point:
This ensures that the player will get to the aiming point without droping hard on the shoulder

**Progressive techniques can include hand shields with actual speed
Live cut drill with players
Utilized on a L.O.S from a run or chase fit to represent cuting for OZ
Large chute boards

C

Crab Drill

Function: To attack a defender, on either call side for quick hitting plays.

Set-up:
1. Partner up on a line with separation between pairs with the offensive player facing away
2. Have the defender shade to either side with or without a bag
3. Drill can also be utilized on a sled

Drill:
1. On command have the player take his proper steps to carry out an effective crab block
2. Explode by uncoiling off the line while shooting the hands towards the attack point and attacking with the shoulder opposite playside. Head remains up. Contact at this point is made on or while in transition to all fours
3. When on all fours crab drive until whistle
4. Perform both ways

Key ponts:
High impact
The defender when not using a bag must give the proper look while simultaneously maintaining the integrity of the drill; this is done by placing the hands on the offensive players shoulders slightly sprawling yet standing erect

C

Iso Drill vs. stem In/on/out

Function: To block a defender that stems right or left

Set-up:
1. Partner up on a line with separation between pairs with the offensive player facing away
2. Place the defender 1 1/2 yds apart and start on a shade out/on/in
3. When installing utilize a bag then progress to no bag

Drill:
1. Pre-start give the defender a direction to stem towards
2. On command have the player fire out and drive block based on an angle of departure
3. The player should quickly establish what direction the defender is moving then respond and adjust while finishing normally
4. Perform against all alignments

Drill 2:
1. Perform this drill to simulate the begining or 1/2 part of a combo for zone

C

Cut-off Drill

Function: To stop penetration and pursuit and to seal backside penetration and cross face pursuit by a down defender.

Set-up:
1. Partner up on a line with separation between pairs with the offensive player facing away
2. When first introducing this drill form fit the offensive player in a good rip fit

When progressing move to a full go with the defender on either shade

Drill:
1. On command (From a fit position ex: RIP LT) have the player step with the inside foot to start the movement for go-2-go
2. Follow through with a go-2-go method
3. On command reset go full go

Progress to full go from a 3pt and 2pt stance
Perform both ways

Key points:
Be sure that the steps are tight (pitter patter) with the inside foot remaining high
Do no overstep on the first step
Have excellent body control while keeping eyes up
If defender tries to pull up and go back door then tighten up
with the same finish

C

Twirl drill

Function: Same drill as above with both players getting the work

Set-up:
1. Same initial set-up as cut-off
2. Form fit each player in a Rip fit with the same arm Ex: (RT to RT)

Drill:
1. On command, full go several times around
2. Perfom both ways

Key points:
Movement should be smooth not choppy
Body control

C

Boards to Backer Drill

Function: To block a LB fast flowing, sitting, or swimming back inside

Set-up:
1. Set up long boards at approximately 45 degrees with partners facing each other
2. Have the offensive player facing away

Drill:
1. On command the offensive player will fire out and attack by taking a bucket step (Check step) over the board while eyeing his target at level 2
2. Upon movement the defender will flow in the same direction simulating a LB
3. When at the P.O.A the lineman will attack the LB to negate cross face pursuit while finishing normally
4. Perform both ways
5. Have the defender flow fast, sit hard at the P.O.A, and swim back inside for different looks
6. **Work cut drill on backers by simulating speed with a run through then place a stand up bag at the end of the board

Drill 2:
1. Crab drill

Key points:
Utilize an excellent run demeanor while climbing to level 2
To simulate a tighter block, tighten the angle of the boards
Alternate position as a coach to stand behind defenders

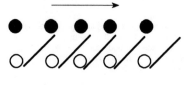

Flat-n-up Drill

Funtion: To climb out of the stance and get to the 2nd level with body control

Set-up:
1. Can be in pairs or groups of 3-4 by simply reducing or expanding the drill
2. Have the defenders stand perpendicular holding a bag on a line
3. If placed in groups set players accordingly, either a bag holder or backer
4. With 1 partner align on the bag
5. With 2 place the defenders 2-3 yds apart

Drill:
1. On command fire out and go full go to level 2 by either Flat RT or Flat LT utilizing the rip or half flipper, while simultaneously maintaining power angles, body control, and an excellent run demeanor
2. Perform both ways before rotating

Key points:
Body control at the L.O.S and at level 2
Pad leverage
Keep eyes up
When clearing defender get eyes to LB immediately

Acceleration Drill (Acceleration Fit)

Function: To establish the angle of departure, read, and aiming points for zone combos

Set-up:
1. Spread players out in groups of 3
2. Start drill with the offensive player to the right covered outside representing an outside shade for zone
3. Look 2 has defender head-up
4. Look 3 has defender inside
5. Can be performed in space or boxes

Drill:
Acceleration fit-has the covered player starting out in fit position (Perform first)
1. On command have the offensive players take one step at a time- Go-2-go
2. On the second command the defender moves in the same progression
3. The third command -go, has the players at full speed to finish
4. Reset then go full
5. Perform drill for all three looks, both ways RT & LT, then switch the covered offensive player

Key points:
Follow through with zone blocking principles
Angles of departure
Keys
Aiming points
Excellent run demeanor
Speed

Zone Covered/Uncovered Drill (Inside/Outside Zone)

Function: To establish the angle of departure, read, and aiming points for zone combos versus 1 defender

Set-up:
1. Spread players out in groups of 3
2. Start drill with the offensive player to the right covered outside representing an outside shade for zone
3. Look 2 has defender head-up
4. Look 3 has defender inside
5. Can be performed in space or boxes

Drill:
**Perform first having the covered player start out in a fit position
1. Give the defender a direction to go-in, hang, or out
2. On command have the offensive players fire out full go
3. Perform drill vs. all three looks, both ways RT & LT, then switch the covered offensive player
4. Rep count should be getting 6 reps for each look, while maximizing time

Key points:
Splits & Communication
Follow through with zone blocking principles
Angles of departure
Keys (hip, pit, shoulder)
Aiming points
Excellent run demeanor
Speed

FULL LINE DRILL

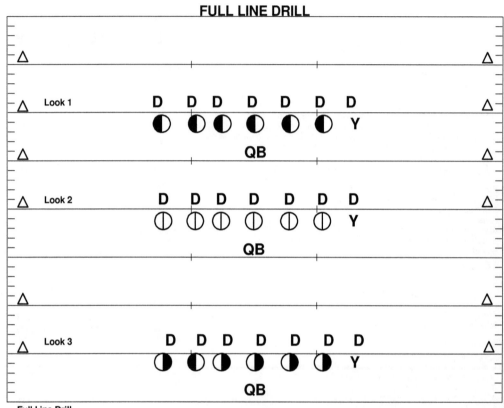

Full Line Drill

Function: To work zone and iso blocks in part then to a full setting

Set-up: Pair up with players 2yds apart across a line. Place 4 cones on 2 lines to start and end. Work drive blocking relative to alignment and play called. Drive progression is performed in parts to full go. Drive 5yds, turn around reset then work back.

Drill:
1. On command, full go
Blocks:

Zone vs. in/on/out
Zone vs. stems
Iso vs. in/out

Zone Drill vs. 2 & 3 (R/T/LB)

Function: To establish the angle of departure, read, and aiming points for zone combos versus 2 defenders

Set-up:
1. Spread players out in groups of 4
2. Start drill with the offensive player to the right covered outside representing an outside shade for zone
3. Look 2 has defender head-up
4. Look 3 has defender inside
5. Can be performed in space or boxes
**Acceleration fit-has the covered player starting out in fit position (Perform first)

Drill:
1. On command have the offensive players take one step at a time -Go-2-go
2. On the second command the defender moves in the same progression
3. The third command -go, has the players at full speed while finishing
4. Reset then go full
5. Perform drill for all three looks, both ways RT & LT, then switch the covered offensive player

Key points:
Angles of departure, Keys and aiming points, Excellent run demeanor and Speed

Zone vs. 3

Function: To establish the angle of departure, read, and aiming points for zone combos versus 3 defenders

Set-up:
1. Spread players out in groups of 6
2. Start drill with look 1 (LB-10, 3T, 5T)
3. Look 2 has (1T, OR 2I, LB-30, 5T)
4. Look 3 has (N, LB's-20)
5. Can be performed in space or boxes

Drill:
1. On command have the offensive players take one step at a time -Go-2-go
2. On the second command the defender moves in the same progression
3. The third command -go, has the players at full speed while finishing
4. Reset then go full
5. Perform drill for all three looks, both ways RT & LT,

Key points:
Communication
Angles of departure, keys and aiming points
Excellent run demeanor and Speed

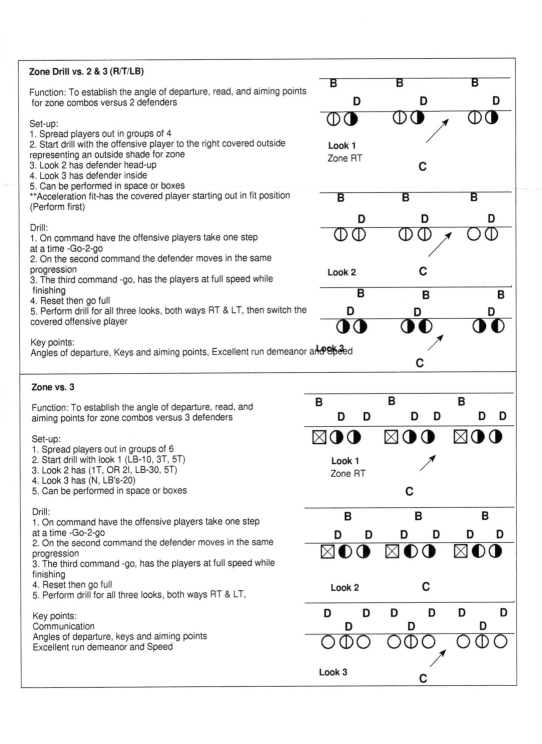

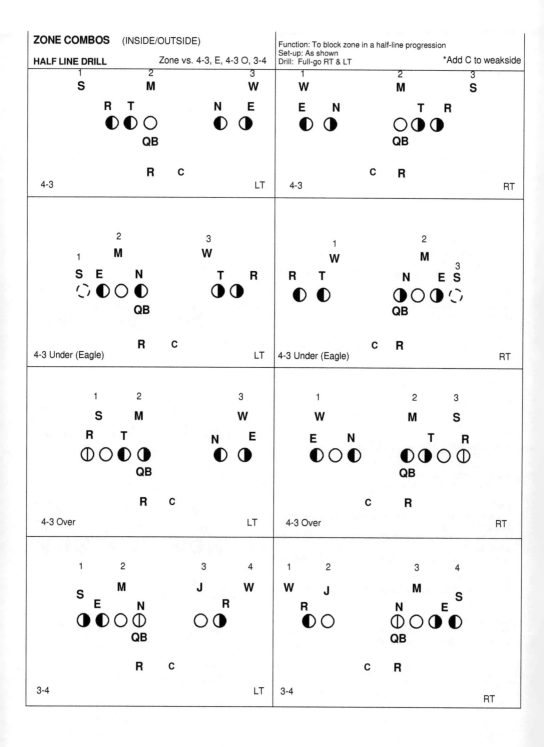

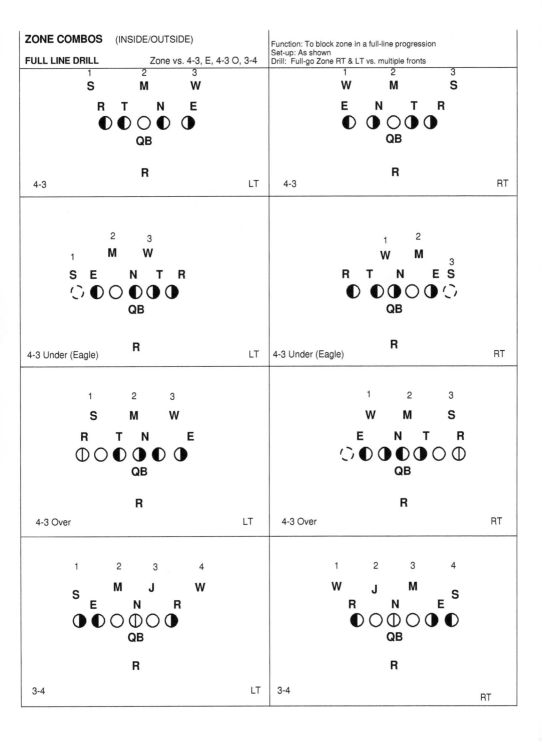

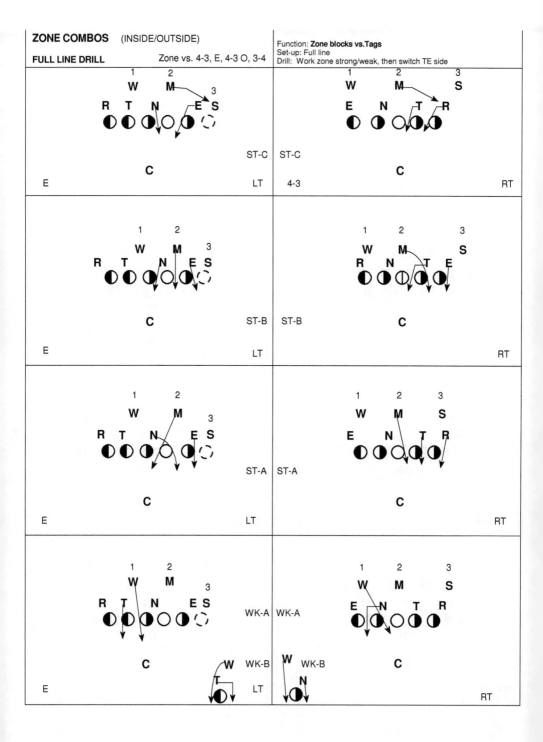

Zone vs. Stunts & games

Function: **Zone blocks versus stunts**
Set-up: Full Line
Drill: 1. Full go inside/outside zone 2. Work zone strong/weak, then switch TE side

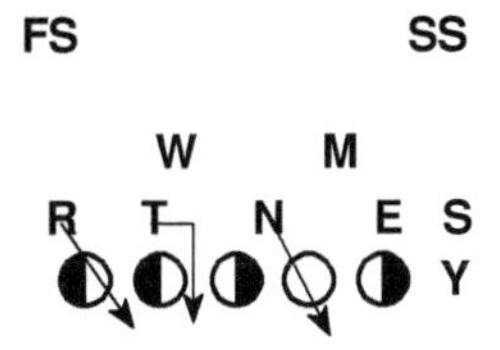

4-3UH (eagle)

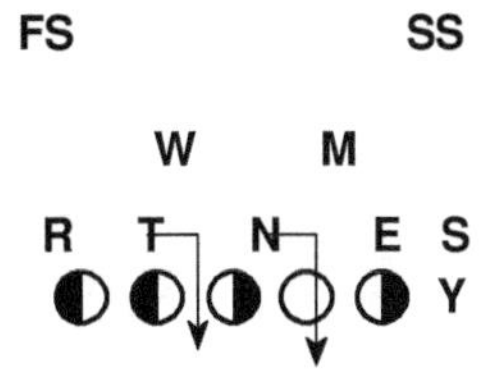

4-3UH (eagle)

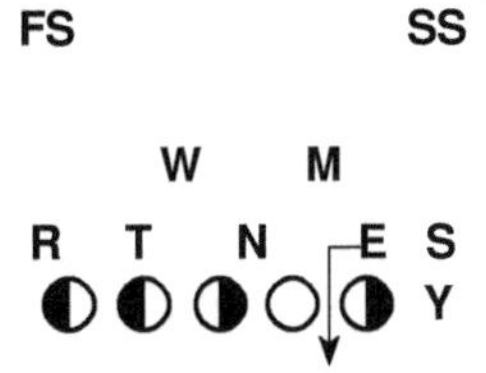

4-3UH (eagle)

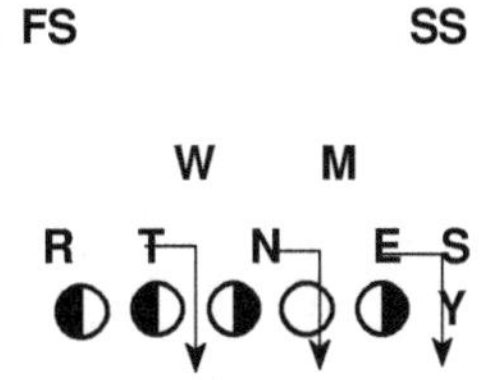

4-3UH (eagle)

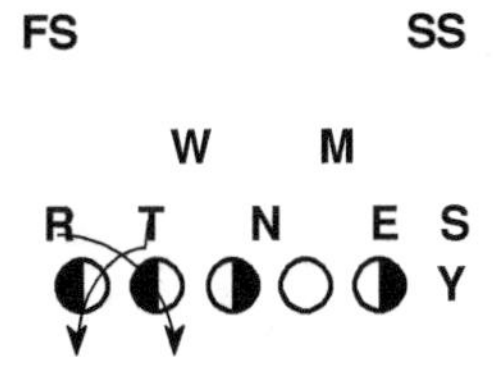

4-3UH (eagle)

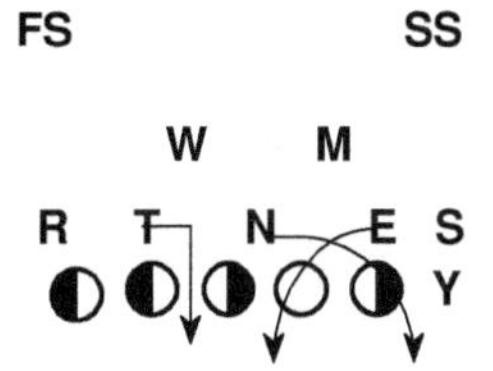

4-3UH (eagle)

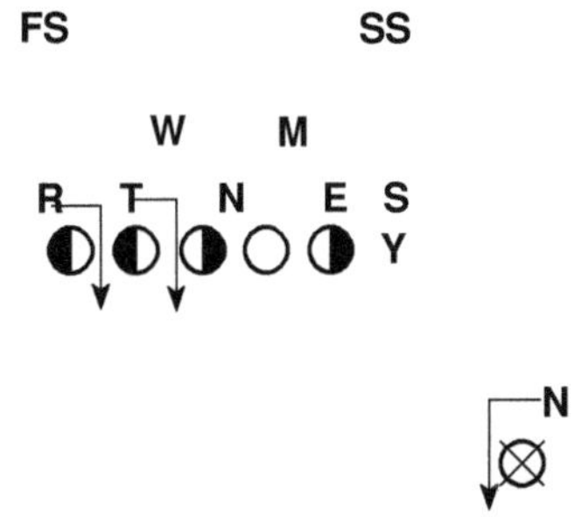

4-3UH (eagle)

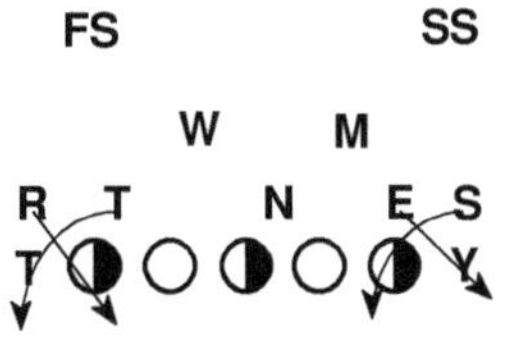

4-3UH (eagle)

Zone vs. Stunts & games

Function: **Zone blocks versus stunts**
Set-up: Full Line
Drill: 1. Full go inside/outside zone 2. Work zone strong/weak, then switch TE side

4-3UH (eagle)	4-3UH (eagle)
*Nat/Tan Twist 4-3UH (eagle)	4-3UH (eagle)
4-3UH (eagle)	4-3UH (eagle)
4-3UH (eagle)	4-3UH (eagle)

Zone vs. Stunts & games

Function: **Zone blocks versus stunts**
Set-up: Full Line
Drill: 1. Full go inside/outside zone 2. Work zone strong/weak, then switch TE side

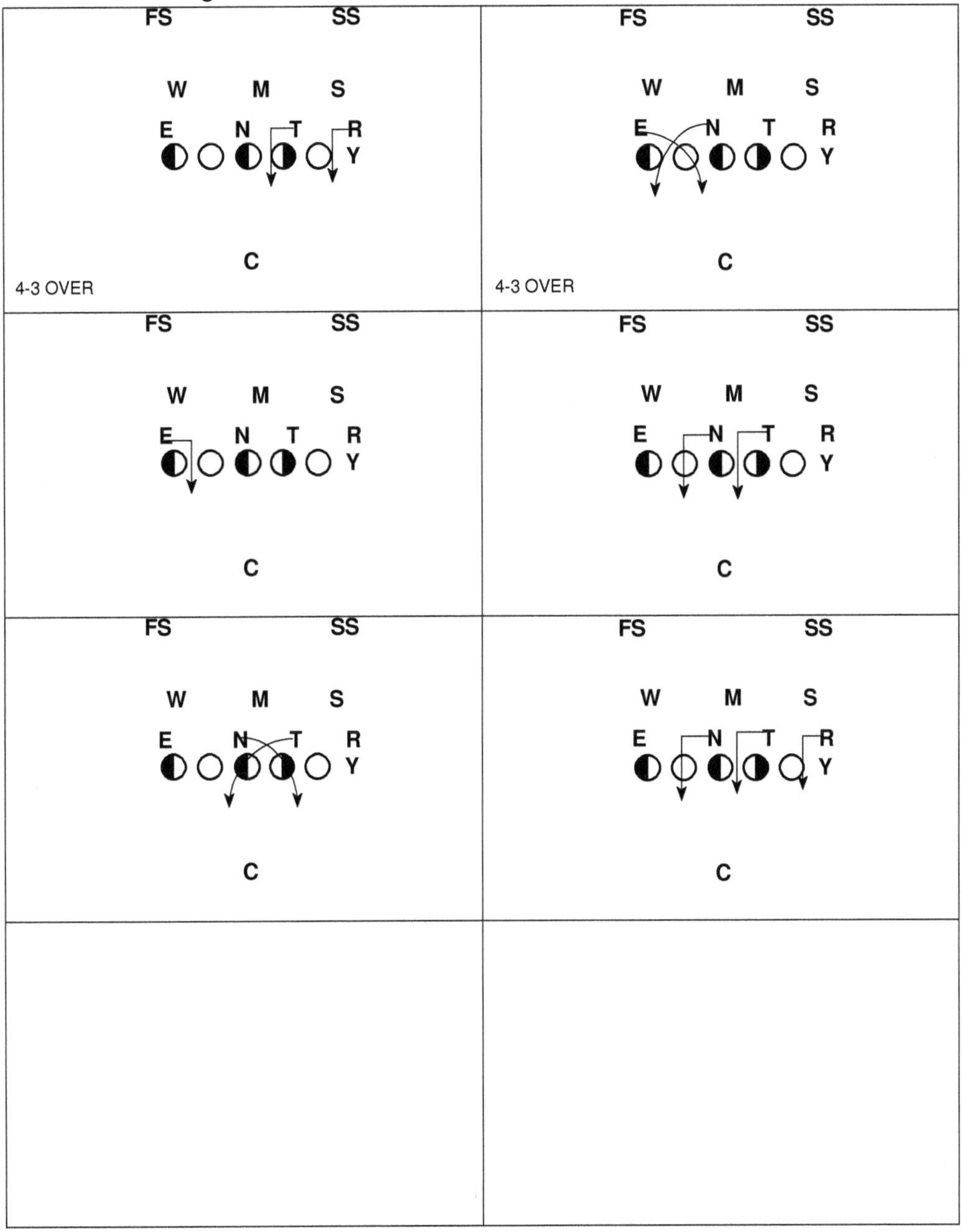
FS
SS
W
M
S
E
N
T
R
Y
C
4-3 OVER
4-3 OVER

Zone vs. Stunts & games

Function: **Zone blocks versus stunts**
Set-up: Full Line
Drill: 1. Full go inside/outside zone 2. Work zone strong/weak, then switch TE side

Post Drill

Function: To block a double team by utilizing hip to hip relationship

Set-up:
1. Start off with a pair of players on a line with a vertical line between them
2. Have the other players align behind them ready to step in
3. Coach will stand behind the players with a hand shield

Drill:
1. On command the players will step in towards each other keeping
their inside foot high (up) while the coach places a bag between their hips
2. There follow through will be climbing vertical while maintaining
a hip-to-hip relationship while simultaneously keeping their outside foot back
3. Drive for 5 yds

Key points:
When stepping the players will have two different land marks for hand placement
to utilize a proper fit without bumping each other out
Maintain a perfect run demeanor with pad leverage

Post Drill VS. 1 & 2

Function: To block a double team by utilizing hip to hip relationship

Set-up:
1. Spread players out in groups of three on a line
2. Place defender between both players
3. This drill can be done in space or boxes

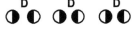

Look 1   C

Drill:
1. On command the players will fire out by stepping T-board RT or T-board LT
 at the defender to obtain an excellent fit while following through with a vertical double team
3. Drive for 5 yds
4. When at 5yds rotate players then drive back
5. Perform until all players go RT & LT

Drill 2:
1. Perform same way while doubling to a flowing backer
2. When contact is imminent the nearest player will punch off and attack LB
while the fitted player adjusts and finishes normally

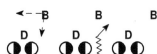

Key points: Look 2   C
When stepping the players will have two different land marks for
hand placement
to utilize a proper fit without bumping each other out
Maintain a perfect run demeanor with pad leverage

PULLING

Trap Drill

Function: To vacate an area and trap block along with working back/down blocks.

Set-up:
1. Separate players on a line, in space, or in boxes in groups of 4
2. Set drill up to work pulling and blocking both ways
3. The defender being trapped should be no more than 5-8 yds away
while the defender should be aligned in a shade

Drill:
1. On command the trapper will fire out utilizing all coaching points
targeted at the defender holding a shield while stepping over a board or line
2. The player blocking back/down will simultaneously fire out
full go and block versus a penetrator, reader, or swimmer

Key points:
Proper pulling techniques
Run through at the P.O.A

C

Pulling Drills   (Trap, Wrap, Boot, G scheme-tight/wide)

Function: To vacate an area and either lead block, seal block, fold block or isolate a defender

Set-up:
1. Place 2 players between 6 cones with a board or line next to their outside foot
2. This drill takes place between 10 yds and has several variations to it
3. When progressing utilize defenders with bags at the P.O.A, as well as obstacles (flat bag or towel) to
pull around or over

Drill:
1. On command fire out utilizing all the coaching points that go with pulling for power, sweep, wrap, or trap
2. Second drill (dashed lines) is sling stepping -2 gaps when pulling
3. When progressing add defenders with bags
4. Perform both ways and in both positions
5. **Practice pining/kick-out/cutting LB's

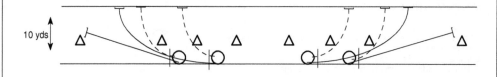

C

Fold Blocking, Draw Blocking, and Counter Pulling

Function: Various scheme blocking

Set-up:
Drill 1:
1. set up groups of 4 on a line or in boxes

Drill:
1. On command fire out utilizing a cross block while working back/down blocking

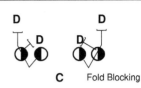
Fold Blocking

Drill 2:
Set-up:
1. Set up a full line with defenders placed in actual fronts

Drill:
1. On command set up and block draw by utilizing the club or wash technique
2. Perform utilizing go-2-go, then reset and go full go

Draw Scheme

Drill 3:
Set-up:
1. Set up a full line with cones placed on an outside shade of the players
Drill:1
1. On command fire out by taking 1 playside lead step before planting and pivoting to pull in the opposite direction around the cone to the left or right

Counter Pulls

Screen Drill

Function: To practice releasing and blocking for screens vs. various looks

Set-up:
1. Utilize 20 yds of open field
2. Place cones in an arrangement of a particular defense to practice against
3. When applicable place stand-up or pop-up bags to cut downfield

Drill:
1. On command fire out and block the called screen by utilizng counts (timing), releases, and proper angles
2. When progressing add defenders to blitz

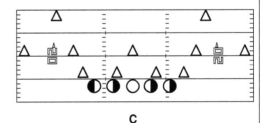

PASS PROTECTION DRILLS

DRILLS

Stance

Function: To properly get into a set position when on the L.O.S.

Set-up:
1. Stack your players to form even or close to groups on a line.
2. On command have the players walk out to form enough groups 5 yds apart vertically by 4 yds horizontally.
3. Start all players in a right stance.
4. a. Set stagger-Toe to instep (can modify) with the inside foot up while toes are pointing slightly outward
   b. Feet align with the shoulders or tighter depending on players height
   c. Roll shoulders back to squeeze blades while flexing chest out
   d. Squat down bringing the chest over the thigh muscles creating the "Z" shape from thigh to foot
   e. With eyes to the sky snap right hand straight out just under chin
   f. Snap it down on the ground with modified wieght applied, fingertips should be flat
   g. Back flat in 3pt, while slightly arched in 2pt

Drill: Can be done by commands or whistle
After setting stagger and upper body-
Commands:
1-snap down
2-hand straight out with eyes to the sky
3-hand down
4-hand up to check for balance
5-hand down
6-freeze and wait to be checked out

Note: If needed have players shake it out and restart thus checking remaining players
Perform both ways.

Power Wave

Function: To teach pass blocking steps with leverage and power angles

Set-up-Same as above with all players in a 2pt stance

Drill: Can be done by commands or whistle
After setting stagger and upper body-two ways to completion

A. Power down for 3 steps then reset
B. Kick slide for 3 steps then reset
C. Then give a direction to start and put it together power down/kick slide for 3 steps
Commands:
1. First perform each step by whistle commands (static step)
2. Rest then go full go
3. Have players switch stagger then redo drill

Key points:
Great stance
Maintain excellent power angles
Balanced and steadied rock
Emphasize pounding the feet into the ground
Control upper body with elbows flexed aimed at the target area
High intensity and high impact is critical

Jam Drill (In/On/Out)

Function: To set and punch vs. all shades

Set-up:
1. Pair up on a line, in space, or in boxes
2. Designate the defenders to a side
3. 1-1/2 yards of separation between partners

Drill:
1. On command step set punch towards the defender
2. Reset then place defender head-up
3. Reset then place defender to the other side
4. Complete vs. all three shades then switch

**Progress to the defender simulating a quick strike, move and 1-2 steps fowards before crossing the linemans face

Jam Set Drill

Function: Same as above

Set-up: Same as above with 1 or 2 hand shields placed on the ground for separation

Drill:
1. Same as above
2. Perform RT and LT
3. Utilize 2 bags for Tackle sets
*Work spin counter

Key points:
Movement
Excellent pass pro demeanor
Timing of the jam with aiming points

Tackles

Interior

LINE-AWARENESS RECOGNITION

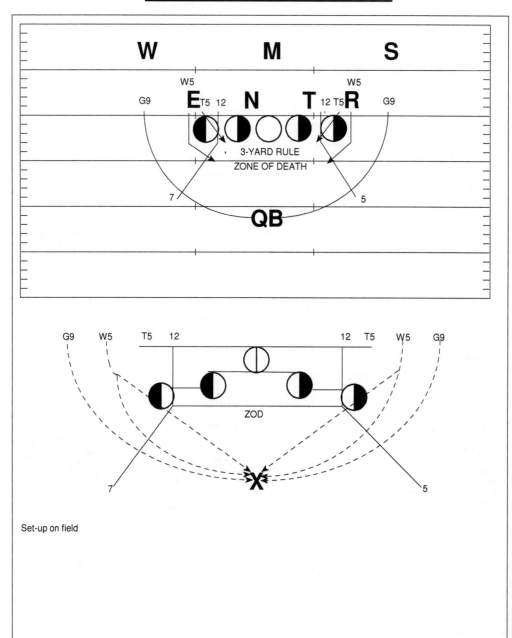

Set-up on field

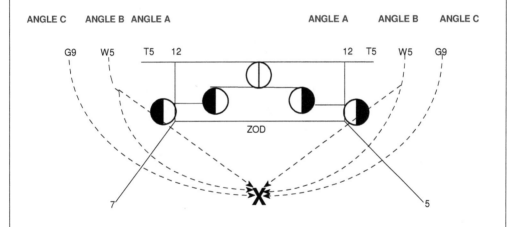

Set-up on field

LINE-AWARENESS SET-UP

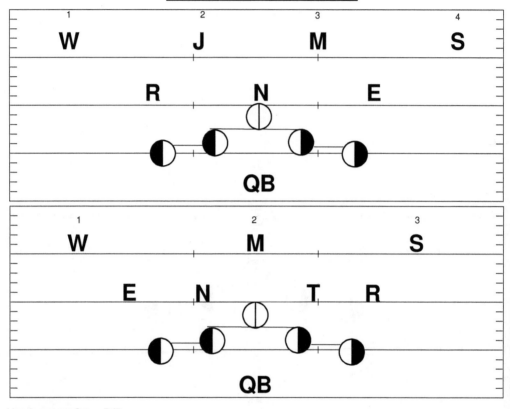

Line Awareness Set-up Drill

Function: To properly set-up in line awareness

Set-up:
Center on the L.O.S. with a normal stance.
Guards-Align the toes of their inside foot on the heels of the center with a normal split of 2-2+feet while staggering their feet (Stance p.16).
Tackles-With a normal split, will align their toes of their inside foot to slightly above the midfoot (opposite the instep) of the guards outside foot. Stances will be 2pt.
Drill:
1. The depth will vary based on the situation (Down & Distance). Shoulders will be square to the L.O.S while the helmet is touching the centers waist-line to ensure a legal set-up. Eyes are immediately aimed at near defender.
*Tackles will have their outside knee narrowed pre-snap while Guards will have a slighter exaggeration in their stagger.

Big Dual Drill

Function: To practice setting while dual reading

Set-up:
1. Set your line as shown
2. Utilize as many players as needed
3. Progress to blitz pick-up

```
     1              2              3              4
     W              J              M              S

              R         N              E
                       (●)
               ◐      ◐   ◐       ◐
                       C
```

```
     1              2              3
     W              M              S

              E    N           T    R
                      (●)
               ◐    ◐        ◐    ◐
                      C
```

Big dual steps
Tackle-will lead with the outside foot first-1-2-3 places him in a demeanor with his inside foot high
Guard-will lead with the inside foot unless read is outside, then he'll lead with his outside foot and slightly widen
Center-will lead back with the foot to the side which he is dualing for 3 steps
All steps finish with their inside foot up while in a perfect pass pro demeanor

Line Awareness Drill

Function: To utilize land marks for various sets versus alignments

Set-up:
1. Utilize 20 cones as shown below
2. A chute board or small board can be placed in front or behind the Tackle
3. The twelve cones inside 6 inches apart vertically
4. Place 5 players in the set-up as shown

Keys:
Integrity of the drill
Stay disciplined to technique from stance to start to finish
Footwork movements in relation-Power-down-Kick slide. Same amount of space covered.
Switch sides and utilize reference points on the field and towards the defender
High impact with intensity while the footwork moves in relation

This drill is designed to condition each player how to defend his pass rush lane while simultaneously reacting to how a defender will approach and adjust in relation to where the QB is. Essentially the defender will tell the lineman where the QB is at.
On whistle Guards and Center will power-down and kick slide to each level of the cone which is placed at several inches apart. Tackles will set to each cone by kick sliding before powering down. The outside and behind cones are set up at 7x7 deep and back to establish a peripheal point for when the QB will be directly behind or even with the tackle. They are reference points for the tackle to understand that he'll hop the hoarse and drive, continue to push defender downfield, or be alert for the defender to redirect and comeback inside either by a spin or club under.

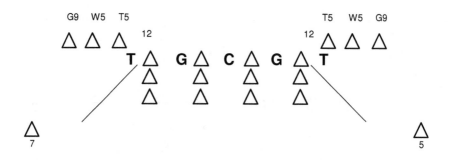

Gauntlet Drill

Function: To practice maintaining a perfect pass pro demeanor when powering down or kick sliding

Set-up:
1. Separate players making groups of 4 on a line with 3 on one side
2. Place a lineman head-up on the player to the inside with his outside foot up
3. Can utilize hand shields or hand pads
4. Can be done in space or in boxes

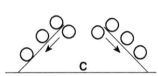
Look 1

Drill:
Look 1
1. On command the player will go full speed by powering down
2. When completed have players move to the other end and power down with the opposite foot

Look 2
1. On command the player will go full speed by kick sliding
2. When completed have players switch sides to kick slide with the opposite foot

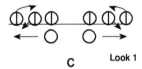
Look 2

Key points:
Center and Guards kick at 2 yds then flat down L.O.S
Perfect pass pro demeanor
Hand placement throughout drill
Speed and exactness
Do not over or under step or lunge

Gauntlet Drill vs. Move/ Stunt

Function: Same drill as above with the player at the end simulating a pass rush move or part of a stunt

Set-up:
1. Separate players making groups of 4 on a line with 3 on one side
2. Place a lineman head-up on the player to the inside with his outside foot up
3. Can utilize hand shields or hand pads
4. Can be done in space or in boxes

Drill:
Look 1
1. On command the player will go full speed by powering down
2. When at the end have the player simulate a designated move then have the player simulate part of a stunt either as a penetrator or looper
3. When completed have players move to the other end and power down with the opposite foot

Look 1

Look 2
1. On command the player will go full speed by kick sliding
2. When at the end have the player simulate a designated move
3. When completed have players move to the other end and kick slide with the opposite foot

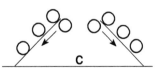
Look 2

Key points:
Perfect pass pro demeanor with hand placement throughout drill
Speed and exactness, Do not over or under step or lunge

Double vs. Pass Rush Covered/Uncovered

Function: To practice setting and slamming a defender when not engaged

Set-up:
1. Separate players on aline, in boxes or in space in groups of 3
2. Designate a player to be covered

Drill:
**2 ways to completion
1. On command have the players pass set while the defender rushes the covered man
2. The uncovered will set, look off then step in and slam the engaged defender
3. Alternative drill is to double by pass setting right away
4. When complete switch covered guys then repeat drill

Key points:
This drill is designed to find work and not stand idle when no defender is present
Utilize indicators

Mirror Drill

Function: To see a proper pass set then mimmick what your partner does

Set-up:
1. Separate players 5 yards apart by 3 yards of separtion in two lines
2. This drill can be done in open space or in boxes
3. Designate a side to have a certain leg high RT or LT
4. Have the man across replicate his partners stance with the exact foot up

Drill:
1. On command the players will go at their own speed to power down or kick slide while their partner mirrors their exact movements
2. Finish when good separation exist or 5 yards have been covered
3. When finished reset, change stagger then perform the opposite way

Key points:
Excellent pass pro demenaor
Timing, it's not a race
Movements are swift and clean
Punch normally while moving
Can utilize long chute boards for L.A. kick sets

Sumo & Sumo Sword Drill

Function: To teach the shooting and snapping of the hands

Set-up:
1. Pair up separating players on a line, in space, or in boxes facing each other

Drill:
1. On command have the players shoot their hands continuously to gain and win inside control
2. On the second command the players will snatch lock and drive
3. Third command or whistle finishes the drill
4. The player who finishes with inside control wins

Sumo Sword
Has the same set-up

Drill:
1. On command the offensive player will punch the defenders chest
2. Upon a firm press the defender will respond by swatting the the offensive players hands down
3. Immediately upon contact the O-player will strike again while the defender swats up
4. Repeat the punch while the defender swats with his right hand down and across the defenders right wrist
5. Repeat, then swap down with the left
6. Complete when several rounds of the 4 movement are performed

Key points:
Integrity of the drill while repositioning the hands
Maintain a balanced and steadied rock

One-Arm Shuffle Drill

Function: To practice a firm snatch hold when hand placement is lost

Set-up:
1. Pair up on a line with separation, in space, or boxes
2. Place players head up on each other with a designated hand in a snatch lock fit
3. The offensive player should be in a perfect pass set with an excellent demeanor

Drill:
1. On command the defender will walk briskly up-field while zig zagging
2. The player on offense will hold his snatch hand firm with the elbow slightly flexed while moving accordingly by powering down or kick sliding
3. When at 6 yds, stop, have the other player fit with the same hand
4. Return and come back
5. Change hands then repeat with the same finish
6. When complete, finish with both hands in a fit as a normal pass rush

**Progressive drill (Brail Drill)
1. Incorporate the offensive player keeping his eyes closed for the entire drill to work the feel and its translation

Key points:
This drill is done at full speed
The offensive player should always remain square to the defender while stepping

C

Sailor Shuffle Drill & Tap-n-Go Drill

Function: To work quick feet, hips, and body placement

Set-up:
1. Pair up separating players on a line, in space, or in boxes facing each other
Have the offensive player set with a stagger while placing his hands behind his back
2. Have atleast 2 yards of separation between players

Drill:
1. On command have the defender zig-zag while the offensive player shuffles and kicks to retreat while keeping the defender square
2. This is quick drill which can easily cover 10 yds
3. When at 10 yds switch players then return

Tap-n-Go Drill
Same set up as above

Drill:
1. On command have the player set and punch towards a designated side
2. Upon the punch the defender will move briskly by zig-zagging
3. The lineman will set and time his jam while powering to kick sliding
4. When finished switch and return

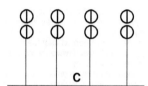

1/4 Punch Drill

Function: Quick feet, quick punch, and change up

Set-up:
1. Spread out and place defenders around the player as shown
2. Start out with the offensive player facing you

Drill:
1. On command have the player chop his feet then give a direction for the offensive player to move
ex: right, right, left, left etc..
Upon every command he'll quickly turn set and punch

Ball Punch Drill

Function: To practice pass setting

Set-up:
1. Form 2 line of players mirroring each other with the same stance
2. Utilize a soccer or volley ball

Drill:
1. On command have the players power down in the same direction while pressing the ball at each other
2. After the first command have the players go at their own pace
3. Perform for 10 yds
4. When at the other side change stance then work back

Key points:
Pefect pass pro demeanor
The ball should not touch the gorund
Maintain approximately 4-5 yds of separation
Catch the ball firmly with thumbs up, then press firmly to the punch ball away
Elbows flexed at all times

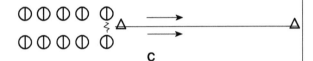

Ball Punch for Kick Slide

Set-up:
1. Same as above, this time one player is kick sliding while his partner is walking him back while

Drill:
1. Same as above with a board
2. Switch and rotate sides when all have gone

Mirror Score Drill

Function: To develop quick feet while not leaning or lunging

Set-up:
1. Partner up and place cones 5 yds apart on a line
2. Place players in the middle facing each other
3. Desigante a defender

Drill:
1. On command have the defender make a quick move, juke, stutter step, or spin on the line
2. Every time he gets punched he does another maneuver while staying on the line
3. After several seconds switch players then restart

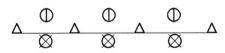

Down the Line Drill

Function: To work flat movement without leaning or lunging

Set-up:
1. Pair up on a line with cones at 5-7 yds
2. Have the offensive player facing away while the defender is set perpendicular with his shoulder fitted into his partner

Drill:
1. On command the defender will begin walking to the other cone
2. The offensive player will quickly shuffle his feet while timing his jam
3. Upon contact the defender will stutter step or juke to throw his partner off balance

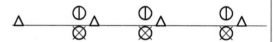

C

Push-Pull Drill

Function: To work balance in a pass fit

Set-up:
1. Pair up on a line, in space, or in boxes
2. Form fit the player into his partner in a perfect pass set with a designated foot up
3. Have the defender grab the player by his inside numbers or with an in-out grip

Drill:
1. On command the defender will either push or pull while the offensive player maintains a perfect pass set while fighting to keep balance as well the defender square
2. Perform for several seconds then switch
3. Perform several times

**Added drill
Same drill
Set-up:
1. Same with defenders grip being over the shoulder and firmly holding the back of the pads

Drill:
1. On command the defender will pull with his right arm while his partner fights the pressure
2. Upon the second command the defender will pull with his left, right, then both

Slide Drill

Function: To work the footwork for slide protection

Set-up:
1. Place 6 cones on a line 1-1/2 yards apart
2. Have the players set behind in a line

Drill:
1. While facing you, on command the player will power forward diagonally around the first cone
2. While in transition he'll follow step, then kick back with the lead foot or foot that stepped first
3. Work to the last cone while having the player face you the entire time
4. When all the way through, change stagger then work back

Drill 2:
1. When completed with drill 1
2. have the players face the cone while increasing their vertical stagger with their upfoot while zig-zagging in and around the cones

Key points:
Perfect pass pro demeanor
Fluent movement with quick transition

C

Slide Protection Drill

Function: To practice slide protecting

Set-up:
2 ways to completion
1A. Start out with one group of players
1B. Make several groups and set them behind while performing the same steps

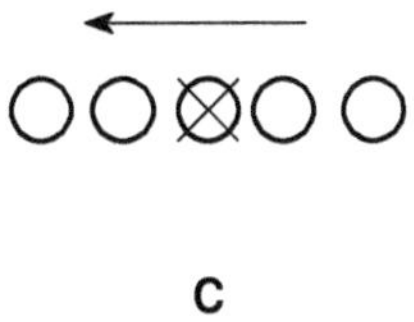

Drill:
1. On command give a direction for the line to slide
2. Perform first with static steps or whistle commands go-2-go-go-etc
3. Reset then go full go
4. Perform RT & LT
**Progress to blitz pick-up

C

Sprint-Pass Drill

Function: To practice changing and moving the pocket

Set-up:
1. Same as above
Drill:
1. Same as above

⟶

○○⊗○○

C

Counters

Function: To drill against all pass rush moves that a defender will employ

Set-up:
1. Pair up on a line, in space, or in boxes
2. Have the defender face you with the offensive player's back to you

Drill:
1. Call out a pass rush move then point in the direction
2. On command have the defender carry out the move while the offensive player pass sets then employs the appropriate counter
3. Go through all basic common transitions
4. Work both ways before switching

Common Transitions

a. Rip outside to spin inside.
b. Rip outside to jump swim outside.
c. Rip outside to jump club inside.
d. Opposite inside to outside for above rip moves.
e. Swim outside to rip outside.
f. Swim outside to rip outside to spin inside.
g. Opposite inside to outside for above swim moves.
h. Bull rush.
i. Bull rush wide to a rip inside.
j. Push to pull, used with swim either way or wash technique.
k. Club outside with swim or rip.
l. Club inside with swim or rip.
m. Double club either way.

Set to stunt vs. stick w/LB follow (Blitz pick-up)

Function: Practice sliding vs. blitz

Set-up:
1. Set up 1/2 line with 2 centers and 4 defenders
2. Place in various shades

Drill:
1. Give backers and down players direction to blitz and stem
2. On command slide to protection utilizing indicators, with normal pass pro finish

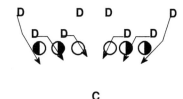

Patience Drill

Function: To develop patience when pass setting

Set-up:
1. Pair up and separate player on a line, in space, or in boxes
2. Place defenders 2 yds away out/on/in

Drill:
1. On command have the player set to
2. Upon movement the defender will move briskly forward
3. The lineman will set and finish normally
**Progressive drill
Move defender back then increase speed

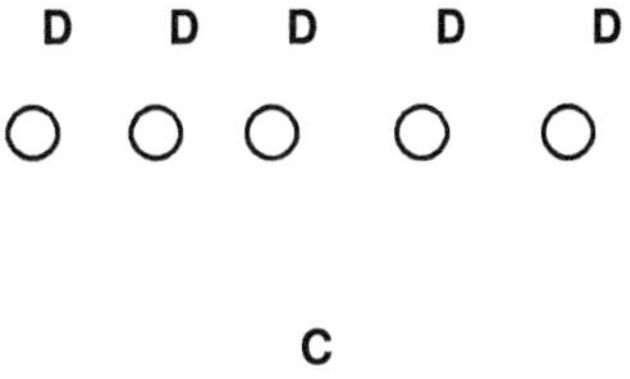

Scoop-n-climb-up-out-back

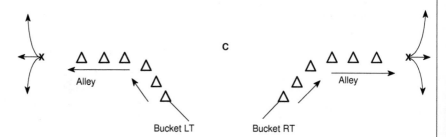

Zone Drill Variation

Place cones relative to the blocker for an aiming point
Run OZ outside the cone and IZ inside the cone
Utilize boards for footwork
Add defender and direction to work steer technique

POWER DRILL

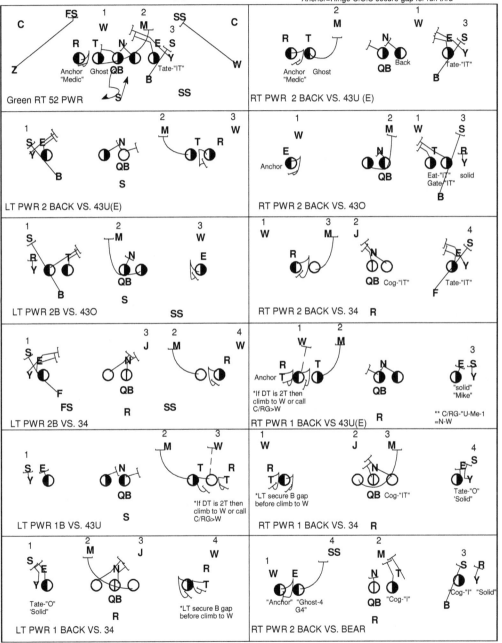

Run Drills:

1. Go-2-go: TB, FL, BKT
2. Strain
3. Firm
4. Flat back
5. Steer Technique
6. Drive-the-bus
7. Fit-n-finish
8. Climb
9. Hip explosion
10. Power strain

11. Cutoff
12. 1/2 man flipper
13. Down & Back block
14. Cut block
15. Crab block
16. Iso vs. In/On/Out...w/stem
17. Acceleration
18. Acceleration w/go-2-go
19. Zone vs. In/On/Out
20. Zone vs. covered & uncovered

21. Zone vs. 2 & 3 defenders (E,T,LB)
22. Zone vs. 1/2 scheme
23. Zone vs. full scheme
24. Zone vs. stunts
25. Zone vs. twists
26. Common leg for double team Iso
27. Bump block
28. Double team vs. Iso and "IT" blocks
29. Oil vs. 3 man tags
30. Trap drill

31. Power drill
33. Draw techniques
34. Folding drill
35. 1 & 2 gap pulling
36. Bootleg pulling w / counter step
37. Screen blocking
38. Cut blocking
39. Pinning and Kick-out blocks
40. Cut off blocking for man and 1-full man

Pass Pro Drills:

1. Pass progression
2. Line awareness
3. Gauntlet
4. Double teams w/ cov & uncovered - slam or lock
5. Mirror
6. One-arm shuffle
7. Sumo & sumo sword
8. Butt block
9. Recovery w knife or butt technique
10. Brail

11. Big dual
12. Sail or shuffle drill
13. Slide protection
14. Sprint pass pro or waggle
15. Alamo
16. Jam vs. In/On/Out
17. Point pec / / Point under
18. 1/4 Quick punch
19. Counters
20. Tap-n-go

21. Power wave
22. Mirror score
23. Snatch lock
24. Ball punch
25. Draw vs. screens
26. Draw and wash
27. Take-two

CPSIA information can be obtained
at www.ICGtesting.com
Printed in the USA
LVHW080543021219
639116LV00009B/248/P